Leonardo da Vinci Topical Study

Lapbook, Books, Time-Line Game, and More

D1666316

Catherine McGrew Jaime

Other Books by Catherine Jaime

- *The Life & Travels of Da Vinci Trilogy (historical fiction)*
- *Da Vinci: His Life and His Legacy*
- *Doing Da Vinci For Kids*
- *Exploring Da Vinci's Last Supper*
- *Lewis & Clark Expedition Unit Study*
- *Amazing Animals Around the World*
- *The Americans Revolt*
- *Astronomy Facts & Fun*
- *New York City Facts & Fun*
- *A Celebration of Black History*
- *Civil War Topical Study*
- *Lapbooking Across Our Wonderful World*
- *Lapbooking Across the United States*
- *Lapbooking Through American History*
- *Lapbooking Through American Government*
- *Learning As We Go: Teaching Through Travels*
- *Sharing Shakespeare with Students*
- *A Novel Approach to Shakespeare's Comedy of Errors*
- *Stars Over Panama*
- *The Adventures of Horsey in Panama*
- *Organized Ramblings: Home Education From A to Z*

Creative Learning Connection
8006 Old Madison Pike, Ste 11-A
Madison, AL 35758
www.CreativeLearningConnection.com

Table of Contents

INTRODUCTION

"Study the science of art and the art of science." [1]

I have been teaching students about the amazing works of Leonardo da Vinci for many years. Students of all ages are intrigued by his varied interests and abilities.

This book includes everything you would need to teach a unit on da Vinic. It could be enjoyed by one or more students on their own, or as the basis for one or more classes on da Vinci. Several of the times I've taught da Vinci, we've done one of the topics here (scientist, artist, inventor) each week. I have also written several historical novels about da Vinci – excerpts from the first three are included here.

The topics within the main portion of the book correlate to different periods of his life – and are laid out in the same chronological order they first appeared in my *Da Vinci: His Life and His Legacy.* I've included a one page overview of each of the periods of his life, so you have a context for them. You may, of course, study/teach the topics in any order you prefer.

Most of us think of art when we think of Leonardo da Vinci; in fact our minds usually go straight to the Mona Lisa or the Last Supper. But da Vinci did so much more than just art. He was an engineer, an inventor, an architect, a mathematician…The list goes on. He was the true "Renaissance man."

One of the many times da Vinci was ready for a change of pace in his life, he wrote a very unusual "job application letter" to the Duke of Milan (see page 71). In that letter he described to the Duke the various types of things that he could do for the Duke. For older students, reading and analyzing this letter can be a great introduction to Leonardo da Vinci.

The map of Italy included in the lapbook shows the places in Italy that Leonardo lived or visited for an extended period of time. (Italy was not a country yet, and many of the cities shown were independent city-states at the time.) And the map of Europe shows several other important da Vinci related locations.

The above was basically my introduction to Doing Da Vinci for Kids, *but it also works well for an introduction to this book, the topical study of Leonardo da Vinci, since my goals with both books are so similar. This book came out of questions about how best to use my materials for teaching da Vinci and the concern about whether there was much overlap (i.e. redundancy) between the materials I have written. Since I have so often taught Leonardo da Vinci as a history topical study, combining the materials I have written over the years of teaching about him into one organized, hopefully easier to use, book was the logical next step.*

---

[1] *Unless otherwise noted, the quotes and the drawings scattered throughout the book are from Leonardo himself.*

"Art truly is a science."
Leonardo da Vinci

Leonardo da Vinci has been described as *"an inexhaustible intellectual energy and curiosity"*
Boston Museum of Science

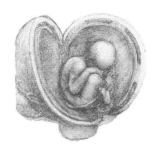

"Many are they who have a taste and love for drawing..."

Note to Teachers/Parents:

This book is intended for students and adults alike.

If this book leaves you or your students wanting more information – there is obviously no shortage out there. I have listed dozens of books and websites in the bibliography to get you started.[2] A couple of precautionary thoughts though:

1. Leonardo da Vinci was accused anonymously of inappropriate behavior during his youth – the charges were dropped; there was no real proof, but some books and websites elaborate unnecessarily on the incident.

2. Leonardo studied human anatomy extensively, and countless numbers of his *drawings/ sketches* show that interest. You may want to pick the books and websites your students look at accordingly.[3] I also take the liberty of "clothing" Leonardo's famous "Vitruvian Man," because the principles he was illustrating are impressive, even if I don't find Leonardo's original drawing necessarily "kid-friendly."

3. Leonardo's parents were not married when he was born. (In fact they would both go on to marry other people.) I do mention that in the section about his family – without going into a lot of details. If you are reading this aloud to younger students, you may certainly skip those portions without losing critical information.

---

[2] *Caution is needed, as noted below, with even these books and websites.*
[3] *I found very few books or websites that could be shared with my students without a fair amount of creative editing first.*

"I've always been intrigued by Leonardo da Vinci, and his artistic abilities. When I prepared to teach a ten-week class on Leonardo, I was amazed at how much I didn't know about him. He wasn't just a great artist. He was also a scientist, and a philosopher. He studied anatomy, architecture, geology, music, mathematics, military methods, and so much more…"

Catherine Jaime

What's Included?

1) Helpful hints to get you started on your own Leonardo da Vinci topical study.

2) Information to make a Leonardo da Vinci Lapbook. Even if you or your students aren't into lapbooking, there is great information included in that section that you can include as you go through the study.

3) Maps, charts, and word searches that can be reproduced for students.

4) Ideas for hands-on student activities for many of the topics.

5) A short, but fairly complete, biography of Leonardo's life.

6) Timelines

7) A Time-Line Game

All of the *Leonardo da Vinci Lapbook*, and the books, *Da Vinci: His Life and His Legacy* and *Doing Da Vinci for Kids* are included here. (The two books have been combined, and duplicate pages removed, but all of their information is here.) Additionally, portions of the first three novels I wrote about him (*The Life & Travels of Da Vinci Trilogy*), the Horsey and Friends book: *Kit and Cathy In Search of Leonardo*, and my short booklet, *Exploring Da Vinci's Last Supper*, are also included.

Getting Started

I have taught the topic of Leonardo da Vinci to students more times than any other particular topic I teach. It is a subject I return to again and again. I have taught an overview of his life and accomplishments in a 1 ½ hour workshop, I have taught ten weekly co-op classes on him, and I have even done a hands-on weekly class for an entire school year. This book comes from the compilation of the materials I wrote for and from those classes.

It's easy, fun, and informative to do a topical study of Leonardo da Vinci. A study of Leonardo is a great tool to introduce students of all ages to the Renaissance (my da Vinci students have ranged from ages seven to seventeen). It can be done with or without the hands-on component, depending on your time limitations and personal desires.

Several important things to remember as you do this:
1. You don't have to do all the work, especially with older students. If you want more information than I've provided here, get them involved in the research. They will learn even more in the process.
2. You don't have to have it all figured out before you start. You will make adjustments in the plan as you go, that's okay.
3. It's okay to not know the answer to something that comes up. (It will make your students feel better about how much they don't know, too!) Looking it up together is a great response to not knowing something!
4. You can do as much or as little with a study like this as you want, and use as many or as few additional resources as you like. We've provided enough to get you started.
5. Everything given here or suggested here is an option, not a requirement. From here you can head in so many directions. Every time I teach about da Vinci, I do it a little differently! The choices are up to you and your students!

There are only a few basic steps to getting started on a topical study like this:
1. Choose your topic – which you've done: Leonardo da Vinci.
2. Decide how long you want to spend on the study: one week, ten weeks, one school year – the choice is yours. Our favorite studies generally last at least two months. Choose your weekly schedule. I like to spend one and a half to two hours, once a week, when I teach a topic like this. When I have spent months on this topic I have generally gone through Leonardo's life in a combination of chronological and topical order, just as the material is presented here. You may, of course change that up, depending on the length of time and your preferences.
3. Do it. Get started, have fun, and see what you (and your students) learn in the process!

Sample Schedule

For a ten week study:

1. Week One: Introduction to da Vinci and the Renaissance.

    The material in the lapbook works well for an introduction - the maps (pages 16&17), the general word searches (pages 18&19), as well as the short timeline of his life (page 21 or pages 36&37-this one matches the game cards).

2. Weeks Two – Nine: Eight topics from the list that follows.
3. Wrap up Session – Favorite parts, Time-line game, etc.

    Each student could give a presentation on one of the different topics you've studied, share their favorite invention of his, about his favorite painting… (you get the idea).

We did the following fourteen topics when we did the yearlong study, spending one to three weeks on each one. For shorter studies, I combined some topics or eliminated some.

"Learn diligence before speedy execution."

Leonardo da Vinci

Leonardo da Vinci Lapbook

Lapbooking Tips

We fell into lapbooking a few years ago, almost by accident. We had stayed away from them because they seemed too complicated and time consuming. But we quickly figured out they didn't have to be. Lapbooking is so great because there are no hard-set rules! It is really whatever works for you and your students! We've used lapbooking in classes we've done – giving the kids all the same materials to work with, and had them each come up with a different end product!

All the lapbooks we've seen/done have one thing in common: A file folder refolded to make a book that can fit in one's lap! Color file folders are the most fun – and can be bought almost anywhere that sells office supplies. From there, the sky's the limit

- We almost always include timelines in our lapbooks.
- Maps are a nice addition.
- Dover coloring book pictures show up in most of ours.
- We often expand our lapbooks with cardstock flaps – to give more gluable surfaces!
- And yes, we occasionally use folds, booklets, and some of the other more complicated lapbooking techniques. (But, not as often as we do simple!)

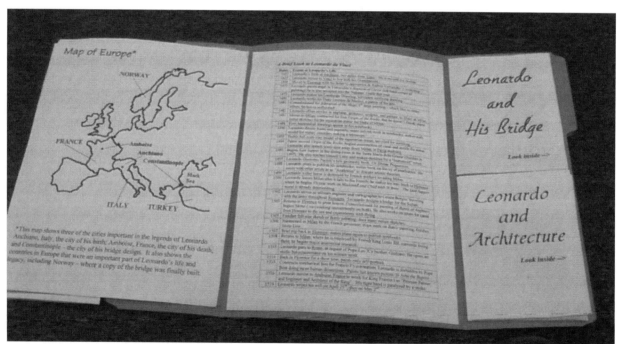

One of many ways to do a Leonardo Lapbook!

Note: We once did the cards (pages 24-31) as back to back little booklets as shown on the right side of the example. But now, we prefer the simpler method of doing each of those pages as four cards that can be cut apart. The cards can be put in pockets on the lapbook where the booklets are shown, or kept separate. They make great matching and sorting games as well. We use lapbooks to introduce a subject, or to bring closure to a study, or for review…We like to copy our masters onto color paper and/or color cardstock – to make the finished product…more colorful!

And of course, you can add additional items – the internet abounds with great printable pictures for almost any topic! So, whether you start with one of our lapbook sets, or make yours up completely from scratch, be sure to let your students get creative with **their** projects!

We designed this set with lapbooking in mind originally, but they all contain great information that can also be used as the basis for notebooking or mini unit studies.

Map of Europe*

*This map shows three of the cities important in the legends of Leonardo: Anchiano, Italy, the city of his birth; Amboise, France, the city of his death; and Constantinople – the city of his bridge design.

It also shows the countries in Europe that were an important part of Leonardo's life and legacy, including Norway – where a copy of the bridge was finally built.

Map of Italy*

*Shows the places in Italy that Leonardo lived or visited for an extended period of time. (Italy was not a country yet – and many of the cities shown were independent city-states at the time.)

Important Places in Leonardo's Life

V	T	N	U	I	A	M	V	R	N	D	L	W	U	X	R	O	A	B	J
K	R	Q	S	C	T	I	A	M	C	Z	I	D	J	G	T	L	G	O	D
A	L	U	Z	D	B	B	I	N	E	V	K	V	J	T	X	R	C	S	S
O	P	W	H	P	N	L	H	N	T	L	Q	F	O	C	V	J	Q	P	C
L	D	R	D	B	A	G	S	E	S	U	D	M	U	F	G	U	E	H	J
A	D	L	K	N	F	J	R	E	C	N	A	R	F	F	K	V	J	O	E
F	N	M	T	J	F	X	O	B	H	N	L	I	S	J	Z	S	G	R	C
A	M	C	A	B	W	N	K	R	E	S	A	C	T	L	F	J	W	U	N
R	Z	W	H	D	D	H	E	M	T	W	N	J	O	A	F	H	C	S	E
X	B	M	T	I	K	H	P	W	K	B	S	U	N	P	L	W	Z	S	R
A	C	N	W	Y	A	I	S	Z	C	V	T	Y	A	S	E	Y	O	T	O
W	V	I	Y	P	R	N	W	J	B	A	R	D	L	T	A	Q	L	R	L
E	C	I	N	E	V	R	O	X	L	G	X	L	G	W	I	Q	L	A	F
B	I	X	N	C	W	U	C	A	Z	K	R	B	Q	E	M	O	R	I	G
E	A	T	I	C	X	F	F	V	W	Y	L	I	B	O	G	F	V	T	I
W	N	P	I	J	I	Y	V	J	D	A	M	B	O	I	S	E	B	G	R

1. Bosphorus Strait
2. France
3. Florence
4. Anchiano
5. Rome
6. Italy
7. Ottoman Empire
8. Amboise

Leonardo's Occupations

R	M	M	G	N	U	Q	D	D	Q	W	F	V	B	H	K	J
I	U	Y	I	G	A	S	Y	A	O	A	I	T	N	F	L	K
L	S	W	I	L	H	I	R	I	P	U	F	G	Z	O	X	I
N	I	X	D	A	I	C	C	P	T	M	X	S	X	S	L	J
I	C	N	C	M	H	T	R	I	V	N	R	I	A	C	V	I
V	I	L	Z	I	W	E	A	N	T	R	G	C	W	U	T	H
K	A	E	T	C	N	F	D	R	I	A	U	C	V	L	N	Z
R	N	E	H	T	G	A	T	T	Y	N	M	I	B	J	F	Z
O	C	O	I	C	X	N	V	L	S	A	V	E	N	E	S	E
T	K	C	Y	R	Q	A	C	I	S	I	D	E	H	B	Z	V
P	E	H	G	U	O	T	C	G	A	A	T	V	N	T	Y	A
L	C	C	B	B	I	O	U	W	R	T	U	N	I	T	A	M
U	K	F	R	T	H	M	R	T	C	C	I	S	E	S	O	M
C	H	V	M	U	Q	Y	I	L	R	H	Z	O	X	I	O	R
S	A	I	A	Q	P	S	R	E	E	N	I	G	N	E	C	R
Q	H	Q	Q	O	T	O	A	F	B	T	Q	Z	B	W	C	S

1. Musician

2. Aviation

3. Scientist

4. Anatomy

5. Engineer

6. Inventor

7. Artist

8. Mathematician

9. Architect

10. Sculptor

11. Apprentice

12. Military Advisor

Leonardo studied:

- Anatomy

  As he learned more about the human body, Leonardo wrote: *"A wonderful instrument, the invention of the supreme master."*

- Astronomy

  "I say that as the moon has no light in itself and yet is luminous, it is inevitable but that its light is caused by some other body."

- Botany

  "A leaf always turns its upper side towards the sky so that it may better receive, on all its surface, the dew which drops gently from the atmosphere."

- Creation vs. Evolution

  "Why do we find the bones of great fishes and oysters and corals and various other shells and sea-snails on the high summits of mountains by the sea, just as we find them in low seas?"

- Geology

  "Mountains are made by the currents of rivers. Mountains are destroyed by the currents of rivers.

- Mechanics

  "Mechanics are the paradise of mathematical science, because here we come to the fruit of mathematics."

- Optics

  "When both eyes direct the pyramid of sight to an object, that object becomes clearly seen and comprehended by the eyes."

- Zoology

  "The smallest feline is a masterpiece."

- and much more…

Leonardo:
- Observed
- Questioned
- Made hypotheses
- Experimented
- Measured:
  - Humidity
  - Altitude
  - Distance traveled
  - Speed of wind
  - Motion of water
  - Intensity of Light

His notebooks also included:
- astronomy,
- botany,
- drafts of letters,
- drawings,
- geology,
- geography,
- geometry,
- invention plans,
- lists of books,
- maps he had drawn,
- menus from what he had eaten recently,
- nature observations,
- notes from borrowed books,
- sketches for paintings he was working on,
- water,
- weapons,
- and work with weights.

Leonardo's plans were varied, including a wide variety of ideas:

- o Automatic Roasting Spit
- o Bicycle
- o Clock
- o Diving Suit
- o Drilling Machine
- o Double Crane
- o Eye Glasses
- o Fan
- o Flying Ship
- o Hang Glider
- o Helicopter
- o Horseless Wagon
- o Locks for Canals
- o Mechanical Drum
- o Monkey Wrench
- o Oil Lamp that gave out brighter light
- o Paddle Boat
- o Parachute
- o Pontoon Bridges
- o Projector
- o Pulleys
- o Revolving Bridge
- o Revolving Crane
- o Self-propelled Car
- o Spinning Wheel improvements
- o Submarine
- o Tank
- o Telescope
- o Temporary Bridges
- o Water Pump
- o Water Wheel
- o Wheel Barrow
    to name "a few"…

A Brief Look at Leonardo da Vinci

Dates	Events in Leonardo's Life
1452	Leonardo's Birth at **Anchiano**, two miles from **Vinci** – He lives with his mother.
~1455	Leonardo moves to **Vinci** to live with his Grandparents.
~1466	Moves to **Florence** with his father to apprentice in Andrea Verrocchio's workshop.
1472	Leonardo paints angel in Verrocchio's *Baptism of Christ* (left hand corner of painting); he is also accepted into the Painters' Guild that year.
1473	Leonardo makes his Landscape Drawing, his oldest surviving drawing.
1480	Leonardo works for Duke Lorenzo de Medici, a patron of the arts.
1481	Commissioned for *Adoration of the Magi*, first large painting – which like so many others, he leaves unfinished!
1482	Leonardo offers service as engineer, architect, sculptor, and painter, to Duke of Milan.
1483	Moves to **Milan** contracted for first *Virgin of the Rocks*, that he doesn't finish; starts initial sketches for the equestrian statue for Duke of Milan.
1488	First Anatomical drawings appear in his notebooks.
1490	Leonardo directs feasts and pageants; starts serious work in notebooks; makes scale model for statue; considers making a telescope.
1493	Builds full-scale clay model of the equestrian statue, unveiled for wedding.
1494	Paints second *Virgin of the Rocks;* begins construction of canal and molds for statue. Leonardo also spends some time away from Milan, in **Pavia** studying.
1495	Begins *Last Supper* in the dining room at the Santa Maria delle Grazie (finishes in 1497). He also teaches himself Latin and makes sketches for a "humanoid" robot.
1497	Leonardo illustrates Pacioli's new geometry book, *On Divine Proportion*.
1498	Leonardo plans to publish his notebooks; writes book on theory of mechanics. He meets with other artists at an "Academia" to discuss artistic theories.
1499	Leonardo's clay horse is destroyed by French soldiers invading Milan.
1500	Leonardo leaves Milan after it falls to the French; he makes his way back to **Florence** where he begins ten-year work on *Madonna and Child with St Anne. The Last Supper* mural is already deteriorating.
1502	Leonardo serves as military engineer and cartographer to Cesare Borgia; traveling with the army throughout **Romagna**. Leonardo designs a bridge for the Sultan.
1503	Returns to **Florence** to great honors. Commissioned for painting of *Battle of Anghiari;* begins *Mona Lisa* (working intermittently on both). He also works on plans for canal from Florence to the sea and experiments with flying.
1505	Finishes full-size sketch of *Battle* painting; does many nature sketches.
1506	Summoned to **Milan** by the French governor; stops work on *Battle* painting; finishes *Mona Lisa*.
1507	Brief trip back to **Florence**; makes plans again to publish notebooks.
1508	Returns to **Milan**, where he is employed by French King Louis XII, currently living there; he begins major anatomical research.
1513	Leonardo goes to **Rome** at request of Pope Leo X's brother, Giuliano. He opens art studio but concentrates on his science work.
1514	Back in Florence for a short time, draws only known self-portrait.
1515	Constructs mechanical lion for Francis I's coronation. Leonardo is forbidden by Pope from doing more human dissections. Paints last known picture: *St John the Baptist*.
1516	Leonardo moves to **Amboise, France** to work for King Francis I as "Premier Painter and Engineer and Architect of the King." His right hand is paralyzed by a stroke.
	Leonardo writes his will on April 23rd, dies on May 2nd.

Leonardo and Nature Studies

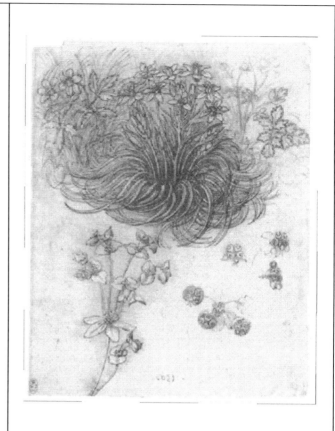

"Consult nature in everything and write it down."

Leonardo and Flight

"Feathers shall raise men even as they do birds…"

Leonardo
and
His Bridge

Top View:

Side View

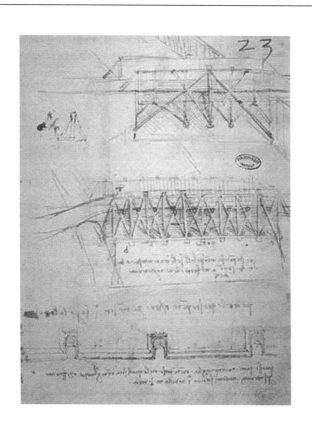

"I have a sort of extremely light and strong bridges, adapted to be most easily carried…"

Leonardo and Inventions

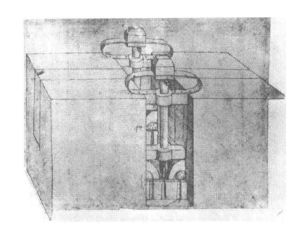

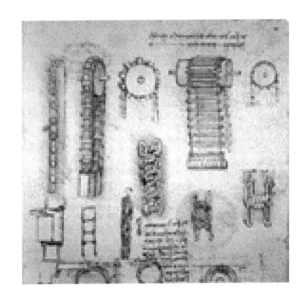

"The perseverance to pursue it and to invent such things…is found in few people."

Leonardo and Art

"Art is a major path to knowledge."

Leonardo
and
Math

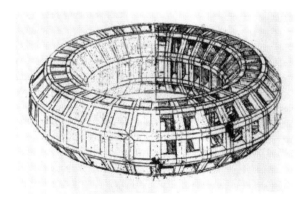

"Mechanics are the paradise of mathematical science, because here we come to the fruit of mathematics."

Leonardo and Architecture

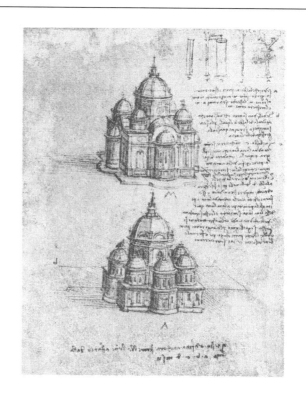

Leonardo's note to himself: "First write the treatise on the causes of the giving way of walls and then, separately, treat of the remedies."

Leonardo and the Horse

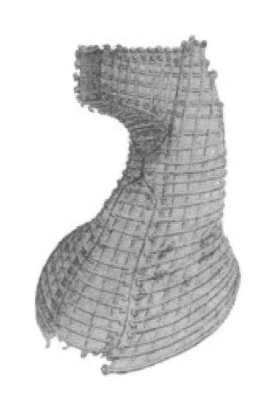

"Again the bronze horse may be taken in hand, which is to be to the immortal glory and eternal honour of the prince your father of happy memory, and of the illustrious house of Sforza."

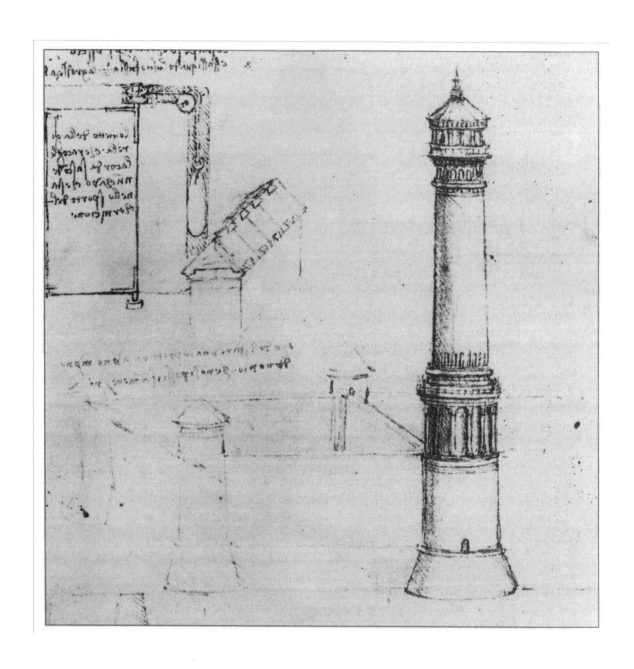

One of Da Vinci's many architectural drawings from his notebooks.

Leonardo Da Vinci Time-Line Game

TIME-LINE
GAME RULES

The game can easily be played by any number of players up to ten. Three to eight players works really well.

OBJECTIVE

The idea of the game is for a player to get eight cards in chronological order in their personal timeline on the table in front of them.

START

Each player starts with one card in front of them face up. This is the start of their "timeline." The remaining cards are face down in a draw pile.

ORDER OF PLAY

The first person draws the top card from the pile and reads the event on it to the player to their immediate left. Play proceeds around the table, one card at a time, in a clockwise manner.

EACH TURN

The "reader" reads the event to the "player" who must guess where that event would fit on his/her timeline. The first time it would just be "before" or "after" the start card. Subsequent times it would be "at the beginning"; "between these two cards"; or "at the end." If the first player guesses correctly, the card is placed in the proper position on their timeline.

If the player guesses incorrectly, the player to their left gets a chance to guess on their own timeline. The opportunity to guess could go all the way around the table to the last player to the right of the reader. (In other words, it's possible for a card to be guessed by all players except the reader.) If no one answers it correctly by then, it is put at the bottom of the draw pile. (With several players that doesn't usually happen, since each player gets to see what the incorrect guesses ahead of them are, each time narrowing the possibilities.)

GAME ENDS

The game is over when the first player has eight cards placed correctly in their timeline.

VARIATIONS

1. For a faster game, a goal number of less than eight can be set at the beginning of the game.
2. When playing with history buffs, it can be required that they give the actual date in order to win the card, not just place it properly.
3. Combine with another Time-Line game.
4. Play with teams of two or more.
5. Have the oldest person read all the cards instead of playing.
6. For a more challenging game, play for more cards required in the timeline.

A Brief Look at Leonardo da Vinci and His Legacy

Dates	Events in Leonardo's Life
1452	Leonardo's Birth at Anchiano, two miles from Vinci – He lives with his mother.
~1455	Leonardo moves to Vinci to live with his Grandparents.
~1466	Moves to Florence with his father to apprentice in Andrea Verrocchio's workshop.
1472	Leonardo paints angel in Verrocchio's *Baptism of Christ* (left hand corner of painting); he is also accepted into the Painters' Guild that year.
1473	Leonardo makes his Landscape Drawing, his oldest surviving drawing.
1476	Leonardo's first younger sibling is born.
1481	Commissioned for *Adoration of the Magi*, first large painting – which like so many others, he leaves unfinished!
1482	Leonardo offers service as engineer, architect, sculptor, and painter, to Duke of Milan.
1483	Moves to Milan contracted for first *Virgin of the Rocks*, that he doesn't finish; starts initial sketches for the equestrian statue for Duke of Milan.
1488	First Anatomical drawings appear in his notebooks.
1490	Leonardo directs feasts and pageants; starts serious work in notebooks; makes scale model for statue; considers making a telescope.
1493	Builds full-scale clay model of the equestrian statue, unveiled for wedding.
1494	Paints second *Virgin of the Rocks;* begins construction of canal and molds for statue. Leonardo also spends some time away from Milan, in Pavia studying.
1495	Begins *Last Supper* in the dining room at the Santa Maria delle Grazie (finishes in 1497). He also makes sketches for a "humanoid" robot.
1497	Leonardo illustrates Pacioli's new geometry book, *On Divine Proportion.*
1498	Leonardo plans to publish his notebooks. He meets with other artists at an "Academia" to discuss artistic theories.
1499	Leonardo's clay horse is destroyed by French soldiers invading Milan.
1500	Leonardo leaves Milan after it falls to the French; staying briefly in Mantua. Leonardo makes a short visit to Venice before returning to Florence; then he makes his way back to Florence where he begins ten-year work on Madonna and Child with St Anne.
1501	Leonardo's cartoon (sketch) for Madonna and Child with St. Anne is exhibited. People flock to see it.
1502	Leonardo serves as military engineer and cartographer to Cesare Borgia; traveling with the army throughout Romagna. Leonardo designs bridge over the Bosphorus Strait for the Ottoman Sultan.
1503	Returns to Florence to great honors. Commissioned for painting of Battle of Anghiari; begins Mona Lisa (working intermittently on both). He also works on plans for canal from Florence to the sea and experiments with flying.

Dates	Events in Leonardo's Life and Related Events Beyond
1504	Leonardo's father dies, leaving behind twelve children, and no will. Leonardo receives nothing from the estate.
1505	Finishes full-size sketch of *Battle* painting; does many nature sketches.
1506	Summoned to Milan by the French governor; stops work on *Battle* painting; finishes *Mona Lisa*.
1507	Makes plans again to publish notebooks. Uncle dies, leaving everything to Leonardo.
1508	Returns to Milan, where he is employed by French King Louis XII, currently living there; Leonardo is asked to make statue for the victor in Milan, Trivulzio. He begins major anatomical research.
1513	Leonardo goes to Rome at request of Pope Leo X's brother, Giuliano. He opens art studio but concentrates on his science work.
1514	Draws only known self-portrait.
1515	Constructs mechanical lion for Francis I's coronation. Leonardo is forbidden by Pope from doing more human dissections. Paints last known picture: *St John the Baptist*.
1516	Leonardo moves to Amboise, France to work for King Francis I as "Premier Painter and Engineer and Architect of the King." His right hand is paralyzed by a stroke.
1519	Leonardo writes his will on April 23rd, dies on May 2nd.
1550	Giorgio Vasari writes his first edition of *Lives of the Artists*, which includes the first biography of Leonardo da Vinci.
1570	Melzi, one of Leonardo's students, dies before finishing work on Leonardo's *Treatise on Painting*. Dispersion of the pages of Leonardo's notebooks begins.
1651	Leonardo's *Treatise on Painting* is finally published.
1652	A door is cut in the wall where the *Last Supper* is.
1800 – 1803	*Mona Lisa* hangs in Napoleon's bedroom.
1911	*Mona Lisa* is stolen. The painting is recovered two years later.
1963	*Mona Lisa* visits the U.S.
1974	*Mona Lisa* is encased in a special bullet proof glass box before she visits Tokyo and Moscow, and then returns to France "for good."
1977	Major restoration begins on *The Last Supper*. The restoration takes twenty-two years to complete. The idea for *Leonardo's Horse* comes to the American pilot, Charles Dent. Twenty-two years later *Leonardo's Horse* is unveiled in Milan.
1990's	A robot is built according to Leonardo's drawings.
1999	A working parachute, based on Leonardo's plans, is built and tried out.
2002	*Leonardo's Bridge* is built in Norway.

1451	~1455	~1466
Leonardo's Birth at Anchiano, two miles from Vinci. He lived there with his mother for his early years. **Leonardo da Vinci TimeLine Game**	Leonardo moves to Vinci to live with Grandparents. **Leonardo da Vinci TimeLine Game**	Moves to Florence with his father to apprentice in Andrea Verrocchio's workshop. **Leonardo da Vinci TimeLine Game**
1472	**1473**	**1476**
Leonardo paints the angel in Verrocchio's *Baptism of Christ* (left hand corner); is also accepted into Painters' Guild the same year. **Leonardo da Vinci TimeLine Game**	Leonardo's Landscape Drawing, his oldest surviving drawing. **Leonardo da Vinci TimeLine Game**	Leonardo's first younger sibling is born. **Leonardo da Vinci TimeLine Game**
1477	**1477**	**1481**
Starts own workshop. **Leonardo da Vinci TimeLine Game**	Commissioned for altarpiece for chapel. (Contract almost passes to someone else when job not completed six years later.) **Leonardo da Vinci TimeLine Game**	Leonardo is commissioned for the *Adoration of the Magi*, his first large painting – which like so many others, he leaves unfinished! **Leonardo da Vinci TimeLine Game**

1482	1483	1483
Leonardo offers his service as engineer, architect, sculptor, and more, to the Duke of Milan, in his now famous letter.	Leonardo moves to Milan where he is contracted for his first *Virgin of the Rocks* (which he doesn't finish).	Leonardo starts equestrian statue for the Duke of Milan. (i.e., he begins initial sketches!)
Leonardo da Vinci TimeLine Game	**Leonardo da Vinci TimeLine Game**	**Leonardo da Vinci TimeLine Game**
1488	1490	1490
First Anatomical drawings appear in his notebooks.	Leonardo directs feasts and pageants for the Duke of Milan.	Starts serious work in his notebooks.
Leonardo da Vinci TimeLine Game	**Leonardo da Vinci TimeLine Game**	**Leonardo da Vinci TimeLine Game**
1490	1490	1490
Sketches plan for a book, *Treatise on Painting*.	Makes a scale model for the equestrian statue.	Considers making a telescope.
Leonardo da Vinci TimeLine Game	**Leonardo da Vinci TimeLine Game**	**Leonardo da Vinci TimeLine Game**

1493 Builds full-scale clay model of equestrian statue, unveiled for wedding. **Leonardo da Vinci TimeLine Game**	**1494** Paints second *Virgin of the Rocks.* **Leonardo da Vinci TimeLine Game**	**1494** Begins construction of canal in Milan. **Leonardo da Vinci TimeLine Game**
1494 Begins molds for equestrian statue. **Leonardo da Vinci TimeLine Game**	**1494** Spends some time in Pavia studying. **Leonardo da Vinci TimeLine Game**	**1495** Begins *Last Supper* in dining room at the Santa Maria delle Grazie (finishes in 1497). **Leonardo da Vinci TimeLine Game**
1495 Sketches a robot. **Leonardo da Vinci TimeLine Game**	**1497** Finishes the *Last Supper.* **Leonardo da Vinci TimeLine Game**	**1497** Leonardo illustrates Pacioli's geometry book, *On Divine Proportion.* **Leonardo da Vinci TimeLine Game**

1498 Leonardo makes plans to publish his notebooks. **Leonardo da Vinci TimeLine Game**	**1498** Leonardo meets with other artists at an "Academia" to discuss artistic theories. **Leonardo da Vinci TimeLine Game**	**1499** Leonardo's clay horse is destroyed by French soldiers invading Milan. **Leonardo da Vinci TimeLine Game**
1500 Leonardo leaves Milan after it falls to the French; staying briefly in Mantua. **Leonardo da Vinci TimeLine Game**	**1500** Leonardo makes a short visit to Venice before returning to Florence. **Leonardo da Vinci TimeLine Game**	**1500** Back in Florence Leonardo begins his 10-year work on *Madonna and Child with St Anne*. **Leonardo da Vinci TimeLine Game**
1501 Leonardo's cartoon (sketch) for *Madonna and Child with St. Anne* is exhibited. People flock to see it. **Leonardo da Vinci TimeLine Game**	**1502** Leonardo serves as military engineer and cartographer to Cesare Borgia; traveling with the army throughout Romagna. **Leonardo da Vinci TimeLine Game**	**1502** Designs bridge over the Bosphorus Strait for the Ottoman Sultan. **Leonardo da Vinci TimeLine Game**

1503 Returns to Florence to great honors. Commissioned for painting of *Battle of Anghiari*; begins *Mona Lisa* (working off and on on both). **Leonardo da Vinci TimeLine Game**	**1503** Leonardo works on plans for canal from Florence to the sea. **Leonardo da Vinci TimeLine Game**	**1503** Leonardo experiments with flying. **Leonardo da Vinci TimeLine Game**
1504 Leonardo's father dies, leaving behind twelve children, and no will. Leonardo receives nothing from the estate. **Leonardo da Vinci TimeLine Game**	**1505** Finishes full-size sketch of *Battle of Anghiari* painting. **Leonardo da Vinci TimeLine Game**	**1505** Leonardo does many nature sketches in his notebooks. **Leonardo da Vinci TimeLine Game**
1506 Leonardo is summoned to Milan by the French governor of the city. **Leonardo da Vinci TimeLine Game**	**1506** Stops work on *Battle of Anghiari painting*. **Leonardo da Vinci TimeLine Game**	**1506** Finishes the *Mona Lisa* painting. **Leonardo da Vinci TimeLine Game**

1507 Plans again to publish notebooks. **Leonardo da Vinci TimeLine Game**	**1507** His uncle dies, leaving everything to Leonardo. **Leonardo da Vinci TimeLine Game**	**1508** Returns to Milan, where he is employed by French King Louis XII, currently living there. **Leonardo da Vinci TimeLine Game**
1508 Leonardo is asked to make statue for the victor in Milan, Trivulzio. **Leonardo da Vinci TimeLine Game**	**1508** Begins major anatomical research. **Leonardo da Vinci TimeLine Game**	**1513** Leonardo goes to Rome at request of Pope Leo X's brother, Giuliano. **Leonardo da Vinci TimeLine Game**
1513 Leonardo opens art studio in Rome but concentrates on his science work. **Leonardo da Vinci TimeLine Game**	**1514** Draws only known self-portrait. **Leonardo da Vinci TimeLine Game**	**1515** Constructs mechanical lion for Francis I's coronation. **Leonardo da Vinci TimeLine Game**

1515 Leonardo is forbidden by the Pope from doing more human dissections. **Leonardo da Vinci TimeLine Game**	**1515** Paints last known picture: *St John the Baptist.* **Leonardo da Vinci TimeLine Game**	**1516** Leonardo moves to Amboise, France to work for King Francis I as "Premier Painter and Engineer and Architect of the King." **Leonardo da Vinci TimeLine Game**
1516 Leonardo's right hand is paralyzed by a stroke. **Leonardo da Vinci TimeLine Game**	**1519** Leonardo writes his will on April 23rd, dies on May 2nd. **Leonardo da Vinci TimeLine Game**	**1550** Giorgio Vasari writes his first edition of *Lives of the Artists*, which includes the first biography of Leonardo da Vinci. **Leonardo da Vinci TimeLine Game**
1570 Melzi, one of Leonardo's students, dies before finishing work on Leonardo's *Treatise on Painting*. Dispersion of the pages of Leonardo's notebooks begins. **Leonardo da Vinci TimeLine Game**	**1651** Leonardo's *Treatise on Painting* is finally published. **Leonardo da Vinci TimeLine Game**	**1652** A door is cut in the wall where the *Last Supper* is. **Leonardo da Vinci TimeLine Game**

1800-1803	1911	1963
Mona Lisa hangs in Napoleon's bedroom.	*Mona Lisa* is stolen. The painting is recovered two years later.	*Mona Lisa* visits the U.S.
Leonardo da Vinci TimeLine Game	**Leonardo da Vinci TimeLine Game**	**Leonardo da Vinci TimeLine Game**
1974	**1977**	**1977**
Mona Lisa is encased in a special bullet proof glass box before she visits Tokyo and Moscow, and then returns to France "for good."	Major restoration begins on *The Last Supper*. The restoration takes twenty-two years to complete.	The idea for *Leonardo's Horse* comes to the American pilot, Charles Dent. Twenty-two years later *Leonardo's Horse* is unveiled in Milan.
Leonardo da Vinci TimeLine Game	**Leonardo da Vinci TimeLine Game**	**Leonardo da Vinci TimeLine Game**
1990's	**1999**	**2002**
A robot is built according to Leonardo's drawings.	A working parachute, based on Leonardo's plans, is built and tried out.	*Leonardo's Bridge* is built in Norway.
Leonardo da Vinci TimeLine Game	**Leonardo da Vinci TimeLine Game**	**Leonardo da Vinci TimeLine Game**

Da Vinci: His Life and His Legacy

(A Biography)

and

Doing Da Vinci For Kids

(Hands-On Activities & Ideas Geared to Students of All Ages)

Note: *The two books have been combined, and pages/pictures that were duplicates have mostly been removed.*

Introduction to *Da Vinci: His Life & Legacy*

Leonardo da Vinci lived at a time when people did not *specialize* in a particular area, like we tend to do today, and his life showed that trend clearly. May this little book *introduce* you to this incredible "Renaissance man"[5] – the artist, the scientist, the inventor, the architect, the fable teller, the cartographer, the anatomist, the mathematician…

* * * * * * *

What makes this book different from others about Leonardo? Why take on a project like this, when so many others have already been written about him? Because, most books I read that were geared for kids had very little information, and those geared for adults generally had too much. I have tried to make this book complete enough to give a good picture of who Leonardo was and what he accomplished, without overwhelming my readers. I have tried to make it interesting for those who may know nothing about Leonardo, and yet still interesting for those who already know quite a bit! I have also attempted to make it interesting enough for a wide range of ages – from kids of all ages through adults.

And I have attempted to place Leonardo in a framework of history and geography, so that we can more easily understand his accomplishments. The books I read about him often referred in passing to where he was and what was going on around him – without giving sufficient information to understand how those locations and events affected him. I have attempted to fill some of those gaps.

---

[4] *Unless otherwise noted, quotes at the beginning of each chapter and the drawings scattered throughout the book are from Leonardo himself.*

[5] *According to the World Book Dictionary, a "Renaissance man" is "a man who is knowledgeable in an unusually wide variety of the arts and sciences" – and it describes Leonardo da Vinci as the "epitome of the 'Renaissance man.'"*

May we ponder the man, the works, and the accomplishments behind the stories of Leonardo da Vinci. May we be touched in some small way by this "Renaissance Man." And may we gain a better understanding of the times in which he lived.

****

Leonardo's life can be divided into four basic periods:
1. The early years
2. The Milan years
3. The travel years
4. The final years

This book is divided into those same four sections. Within each section, I have included chapters that deal with the different topics that were an important part of Leonardo's life during those time periods.

Leonardo in Western History

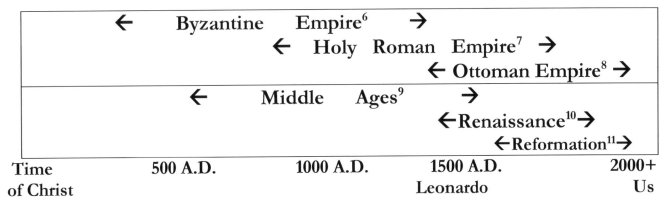

| Time of Christ | 500 A.D. | 1000 A.D. | 1500 A.D. Leonardo | 2000+ Us |

Leonardo da Vinci came into this world in 1452, at a time of great changes in the West:[12] The printing press had just been invented, and so had mirrors as we think of them. The Middle Ages were coming to an end, the Renaissance was in full swing, and the Reformation was about to begin. Even architecture was changing, as domes were becoming more popular, due to the influence from *"the East."*

Dates:	Related/Major World Events:
Mid 1100's to ~1400	Gothic period in Art and Architecture. *(So named by Renaissance humanists, referring to the "barbaric" art of the Middle Ages.)*
Mid 1300's	Renaissance begins in Italy.
1440	Printing Press is invented in Germany.
1452	Ottoman Sultan starts charging ships entering the Black Sea.
1453	Constantinople finally falls, bringing an end to the dying Byzantine Empire, *and strengthening the Ottoman Empire.*

---

[6] *Byzantine Empire was ~330 to 1453 (from the establishment of Constantinople to its fall).*

[7] *Holy Roman Empire – from Charlemagne, ~800, to the end of the Hapsburg line, ~1800.*

[8] *Ottoman Empire – from ~1300 – 1922.*

[9] *The period of time we call the Middle Ages lasted almost 1000 years, starting with fall of the Roman Empire in the 5th century.*

[10] *The Renaissance began in the region of Italy ~1350, spreading across Europe from there, and ending ~1550.*

[11] *The Protestant Reformation lasted most of the 16th century.*

[12] *Here "the West" refers to Europe, parts of Africa, and eventually North and South America and "the East" refers to the Orient and what we now call "the Middle East."*

Early Years – Overview

Leonardo da Vinci was born at the height of the Renaissance in Italy. His early years were not particularly easy for him – he lived first with his mother, and then with his grandparents and uncle, and eventually with his father – changing locations each time. His formal education was very limited until he moved to Florence[13] with his father to apprentice with one of the greatest early artists of the Renaissance, Andrea del Verrocchio.

In addition to this great introduction to art, Leonardo was introduced to Renaissance architecture at this time. Domes were becoming popular in the West, first appearing in Florence, where Leonardo da Vinci spent so much of his early life. In fact, Donato Bramante, one of the greatest dome architects of their day, was working in Florence while Leonardo was there, and Leonardo interacted regularly with him.

In 1472, while still an apprentice, Leonardo was accepted into the local painters' guild. Leonardo continued as Verrocchio's apprentice for a while even after obtaining his status as a "true" painter. In 1477, at age twenty-five, he finally opened his own studio, where he would have many of his own students.

---

[13] *Florence was a fairly powerful city-state in northern Italy at the time.*

Early Years - Leonardo's Family

"He would have been very proficient at his early lessons if he had not been so volatile and unstable; for he was always setting himself to learn many things only to abandon them almost immediately."

-- Vasari

Most biographies list Leonardo da Vinci's birthplace as the village of Vinci, though it is believed that he was actually born in the nearby smaller village of Anchiano.[14] At that time Vinci and Anchiano were part of the city-state of Florence, not the country of Italy.[15]

Da Vinci's home in Anchiano

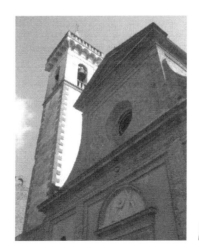 

The Church of Santa Croce (Holy Cross) where Leonardo was baptized.

---

[14] *Anchiano is harder to find on a map of Italy than Vinci is; it is about a forty minute uphill hike from Vinci!*

[15] *Italy would not become a kingdom (a united country) until 1861.*

Leonardo lived in Anchiano with his mother Caterina for the first few years of his life.[16] Very little is known about Leonardo's mother, who is presumed to have been a peasant, since his father did not marry her.

It appears that Leonardo moved in with his father's family when his mother married a few years later. His father's family was from Vinci, and Leonardo spent most of his pre-teen years with his uncle and grandparents at their country estate there. His father, Ser Piero, was a notary,[17] like his father and his father's father. Because Leonardo's parents were not married, the notary guild and the university[18] would be closed to him as he grew up.

Leonardo's formal education consisted of learning to read, write, and do basic math, all taught by the local parish priest. Throughout his life Leonardo referred to himself as "a man without an education." And yet, even though his formal education ended early, Leonardo was always studying and learning. He lived at a time when the newly invented printing press[19] and cheaper paper were finally making books affordable. Over the years, though he was never a rich man, he owned many of his own books, and borrowed frequently from others. His quest for knowledge was never satiated.

Leonardo's father died at age seventy-seven in 1504, with twelve children, ages six to fifty-two.[20] He had been married four times. There was no will, and Leonardo's half-siblings made sure he didn't get any of the inheritance. Leonardo's uncle died three years later, leaving everything to Leonardo. The siblings fought their uncle's will, the court ruled in their favor, and said that Leonardo could only **use** the property until he died, when his siblings would get it! In addition to the financial burden each of these legal fights caused him, and the time the fighting took him away from his work; the larger pain to Leonardo was in being shut out, again and again, from his family.

Leonardo never married – he was seemingly more interested in his work than in establishing additional family relationships.

---

[16] *And she lived with him for the last few years of her life.*

[17] *A notary was a member of the legal profession.*

[18] *A guild was an organization that craftsmen and professionals had to belong to in the Middle Ages in order to do certain types of work.*

[19] *In the West, that is!*

[20] *Leonardo was the oldest by many years, since his father's first two wives bore him no children before they died.*

Early Years - Leonardo, the Apprentice

Leonardo first moved to Florence with his father as a young teenager. At that time, Florence was the cultural center of Europe – ruled by the Medici family, the richest family in Italy.

Leonardo was to apprentice there to Andrea del Verrocchio, one of the most renowned artists of the day.[21] As an apprentice his first tasks were to make paintbrushes, to prepare canvases, and to learn how to mix paints. And like the other artists of his day, he then learned to make sculptures; to make patterns for tapestries and carpets; to paint banners for festivals; to make sets and costumes for pageants; and of course, to paint pictures. He also began to study architecture during his time in Florence.

Painting was not a prestigious occupation during the Middle Ages and the early Renaissance period. Painters were of fairly low status. Paintings were generally done only on commission for those who had money – such as government officials and churches. In fact, paintings were usually done by studios as "group efforts" with multiple artists working on several paintings at the same time. This is one of the reasons most paintings from that era are not signed.[22]

In 1472, Leonardo's teacher, Verrocchio, had done most of a painting of St. John baptizing Jesus for the *Baptism of Christ* painting. He had Leonardo finish it – Leonardo added the angel in the left corner. According to legends, the angel was so much better than what Verrocchio had painted, that Verrocchio said he would never paint again![23]

---

[21] *In fact as a sculptor, Verrocchio had no peers during his lifetime. Leonardo apprenticed with Verrocchio with several other young men, for six to ten years.*

[22] *Up until this time, even when only one artist painted a picture, he didn't generally sign it, since there was no "pride" associated with the finished product. It was just an assignment to complete.*

[23] *It would have been a sound economic decision for the master – since he could leave the painting to his young apprentice, and concentrate on other money-making aspects of his business, such as sculpting.*

Verrocchio's Painting, the Baptism of Christ, *with Leonardo's angel in the left corner.*

Leonardo's oldest drawing, the landscape shown on the previous page, was drawn at this time, also. It is possibly the oldest landscape drawing in the West. In the East, landscape drawings were already very popular, but western artists did only portraits and religious scenes prior to this time.

Early Years - Leonardo, the Architect

Leonardo addressed the damages to a church structure, the St. Francesco al Monte. He also drew up plans for lifting yet another church, and putting a basement under it. He almost convinced the city planners to try his plan.

When the dome of another nearby church collapsed, Leonardo's interest in the strength and safety in buildings was piqued. One of Leonardo's architectural suggestions was to put a dance hall only on the bottom floor of a building, so that no one could be crushed beneath it if the weight and stress of the dancing became too much. He studied cracks in walls, and their causes. He studied the strength of building materials, domes, foundations, supports, beams, etc. He wrote of "the nature of the arch," and investigated what gave it its strength. Leonardo's plans were varied – from churches to palaces to stables, to canals and locks. While his plans for most of those remained primarily at the plan level, some of his research and planning in locks and canals was actually carried out in his lifetime.

While most of Leonardo's architectural work was theoretical and not physical (or necessarily practical) he still contributed much to the field of architecture, with his studies, ideas, and his regular contact with the great architects of the day.[24] His notebooks contain such a wealth of information from this time frame that they almost fully cover the evolving High Renaissance styles of his day. We don't have any evidence that any of the buildings built during this time were fully designed by Leonardo da Vinci, but there are indications that he influenced many of them.

---

[24] *Leonardo served almost in an "advisory" capacity to several of them.*

LEONARDO,
THE ARCHITECT

(Doing Da Vinci)

Leonardo's note to himself:
"First write the treatise on the causes of the giving way of walls
and then, separately, treat of the remedies."

Student Activities

We discussed architectural styles (information on the following pages) and some of the problems da Vinci was concerned about (cracks, foundations, etc.). We looked at many of his architectural drawings (churches, palaces, canals, locks, cities, and more). The students were directed to use any combination of cardboard, paper, straws, toothpicks, popsicle sticks, paper towel rolls, paper plates and coffee filters to design and make their own building.

Architectural Styles before Da Vinci

1050 – 1250 Romanesque Styles in Architecture

The first European architectural style developed. Romanesque buildings tended to be heavy, with a very gloomy appearance, often with towers at both ends.

1250 – 1500 Gothic Styles

The Gothic style developed towards the end of the Middle Ages. Gothic buildings were taller, and more graceful. Stained glass windows were popular.

Architecture Approaching & During Da Vinci's Lifetime

At the beginning of the 15th century, architecture came to be considered the **supreme** form of art. Symmetry and other geometric balance were important to Renaissance architects, as well as classical proportions. **Domes** became an important part of architecture, starting with Filippo Brunelleschi's work on the dome for the Santa Maria del Fiore in Florence. Brunelleschi developed a new type of dome, in order to make it such a large size. The church was completed in 1432.

Santa Maria del Fiore in Florence(Brunelleschi's Dome)

In 1447 Pope Nicolas V commissioned work to be done on a new and improved St. Peter's Basilica in Rome. The first architect to work on it was Leon Battista Alberti, but the work was not completed for almost 150 years.

St Peter's Basilica in Rome

Leonardo, the Architect

From Leonardo's youth, he was fascinated by severe weather – tornados, earthquakes, and the like. He did countless drawings showing the effects of severe storms. Even his architectural studies took weather into consideration – he was intent on planning buildings so that they were strong enough to withstand earthquakes:

> *"That beam which is more than twenty times as long as its greatest thickness will be of brief duration and will break in half...Each beam must pass through its walls and be secured beyond the walls with sufficient chaining, because in consequence of earthquakes the beams are often to seen to come out of the walls and bring down the walls and floors.."*

In the days of da Vinci, architecture was considered a nobler pursuit than painting was, so it is no surprise that da Vinci was also interested in architecture. In his role as an architect, Leonardo's plans were varied – from churches and palaces, to stables, to canals and locks.

While his plans for most of those remained primarily at the plan level, some of his research and planning in locks and canals was actually carried out in his lifetime.

This is Leonardo's Lock in Milan.

In 1483, Leonardo offered his services to Duke Ludovico of Milan as an engineer, architect, sculptor and painter.

In 1485 and 1486 plagues devastated Milan, killing thousands. In the aftermath, Leonardo collaborated with the Duke to rebuild the city. His plans included ideas for a system of water flowing through the city to improve sanitation.[25] He also drew plans for two sets of streets, one for "vehicles" and one for pedestrians.

"By the high streets no vehicles and similar objects should circulate, but they are exclusively for the use of gentlemen. The carts and burdens for the use and convenience of the inhabitants have to go by the low ones."

"Let such a city be built near the sea or a large river in order that the dirt of the city may be carried off by the water."

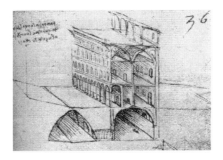

Da Vinci was constantly refining his ideas for how churches should be built. In 1490 Leonardo was sent to Pavia by Duke Ludovico to inspect work on the cathedral there.

He also studied cracks in walls, and their causes.

Note to himself: *"First write the treatise on the causes of the giving way of walls and then, separately, treat of the remedies…That wall which does not dry uniformly in an equal time, always cracks."*

---

[25] *Actually a good idea, but never put into effect.*

He studied the strength of building materials, domes, foundations, supports, beams, etc. He wrote of "the nature of the arch," and investigated what gave it its strength:

"An arch is nothing other than a strength caused by two weaknesses; for the arch in buildings is made up of two segments of a circle, and each of these segments being in itself very weak desires to fall, and as the one withstands the downfall of the other of the two weaknesses are converted into a single strength."

Back in Milan, while Leonardo was working on the *Last Supper*, he could observe Donato Bramante, the court's architect, working on the dome of Santa Maria delle Grazie.

When the dome of another nearby church collapsed, Leonardo's interest in the strength and safety in buildings was piqued.

In 1500, back in Florence, Leonardo was used as an architectural expert in a committee addressing the damages to a church structure, the San Francesco al Monte.

While in Florence, according to his biographer, Giorgio Vasari, Leonardo drew up plans for lifting Church of San Giovanni , and putting a basement under it. He almost, but not quite, convinced the city planners to try his plan.

Another one of Leonardo's architectural suggestions was to put a dance hall only on the bottom floor of a building, so that no one could be crushed beneath it if the weight and stress of the dancing became too much.

He said of foundations:

> *"The first and most important thing is stability. As to the foundations and other public buildings, the depths of the foundations must be at the same proportions to each other as the weight of material which is to be placed upon them."*

In 1503, da Vinci worked on a canal to connect Florence to the sea.

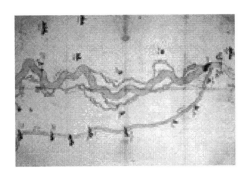

While traveling with Cesare Borgia in 1512, da Vinci served as his military architect and general engineer.

Map of Imola created by da Vinci for Cesare Borgia.

In 1516 da Vinci left Italy for France, to become the "first painter, architect, and mechanic of the King."

So, as you can see, his career as an architect was long and varied.

Da Vinci's *Lady with an Ermine*

Early Years - Leonardo, the Artist

"...art is a major path to knowledge."

Leonardo da Vinci was left-handed, but he actually painted on occasion with both hands.[26] Da Vinci often worked from clay models when he was in the studio painting or from the sketches in his notebooks. He did sketches with red chalk, black chalk, pen and ink, charcoal, and silverpoint.[27]

He considered art to be the "queen of all sciences." He took a small sketchbook with him everywhere. He frequently drew and studied the things around him. He advised his students: "When you go out for a walk, see to it that you watch and consider men's postures and actions as they talk, argue, laugh or scuffle together; their own actions and those of their supporters and onlookers, and make a note of these with a few strokes in your little book which you must always carry with you."

Like many other artists of the day, Leonardo worked on sculptures in addition to his paintings. Unfortunately, we have no evidence that any of his sculptures still exist.[28]

Leonardo learned to paint with the new Flemish technique, which used powdered colors mixed with oil instead of water. The large paintings generally began with:
1. Small sketches
2. Then actual size drawings
3. Then the transfer (holes through the drawing, almost like a "dot-to-dot")
4. Then the dark colored underpainting, which gave the pictures their depth
5. And finally, the bright colors

---

[26] *Michelangelo was also capable of painting with both hands, and would often surprise visitors when he was painting his ceiling frescoes, by switching hands.*

[27] *Silverpoint was a popular way of drawing for Renaissance artists. They sketched first with charcoal, and then applied silverpoint (actually a silver pencil) over the charcoal. A small silverpoint drawing by Leonardo sold for $11 million in 2001.*

[28] *And no evidence that he did a significant number of them either. He considered sculpting to be inferior to painting.*

Leonardo is credited with two new techniques which would change painting drastically, *chiaroscuro* – which deals with light and shade, and *sfumato* – which deals with blending colors/softening around the edges, almost a haze. Filippo Brunelleschi had recently developed rules for perspective in paintings, and Leonardo worked to incorporate perspective into his paintings as well.[29]

From his own painting experiences, Leonardo developed numerous rules and concepts for painters that he cited in his Notebooks. One of his "rules" was: "The mind of the painter should be like a mirror which always takes the color of the thing that it reflects, and which is filled by as many images as there are things placed before it." Leonardo hoped to compile these notes into a book someday. He was personally unsuccessful, but eventually his notes were compiled into the book, *Treatise on Painting*, which was finally published in 1651.

This is the first painting believed to have been done by Leonardo da Vinci, at least that still exists: the Portrait of Ginevera de Benci; he painted it around 1474.[30]

The following is a fictional, but well-researched description of him making that painting from *Leonardo the Florentine*:

> By this time, Leonardo was already moving on to yet another project. He had received his first commission to do a secular work, a portrait. As he prepared to sketch the young Ginevra, he wondered whether she was truly happy. As a member of the Benci family, one of the wealthiest families in Florence, she had everything she could ever desire, at least in the material sense. Yet as Leonardo worked on his sketches of this sixteen-year-old, who had recently been married, he sensed a sadness or melancholy air about her.

---

[29] *Perspective gave paintings from the 15th century a much more realistic look than paintings from prior centuries.*

[30] *Most of Leonardo's paintings were of young women and many of those were "Madonnas" (Mary and baby Jesus).*

She was lost in her thoughts as he drew, and seldom spoke. He disturbed her only when he had to ask her to move slightly, in order that he would have a better angle, or better light.

He was having her pose outdoors, in one of his favorite places to sketch. He would come back in a few days and sketch the juniper bush that would be behind her, the trees, and the other parts of nature that would eventually make up the background of the painting. As he sketched, his mind was already moving on to the next stages of the painting. When he was done here, he would finish preparing the wood panel, and choose the colors. When he started the actual painting he would have her come back for some additional posing sessions. He wanted to be sure that he did justice to her beauty, and the pensive expression that she always wore. He was glad that he had chosen to paint her portrait with the oil paints that gave him much more flexibility in depicting shadows and showing depth.

When the painting was finally complete, Leonardo added Latin words to the back of the finished panel: "Virtutem Forma Decorat" ("Beauty Adorns Virtue"). They seemed an appropriate way to sum up the subject of his first portrait painting.

Unfortunately, he left most of his paintings unfinished over the years. He would give up on paintings at any point in the process when he got bored with them, or became interested in something else. In his desire to be as accurate as possible, he was constantly moving into side interests — anatomy, botany, engineering, and more. Those other interests would often take him away from painting for quite a while. For all the fame attached to his painting, Leonardo completed many more sketches than he did paintings. Modern historians believe he only finished about twenty-five paintings in his lifetime, and less than twenty of those still exist today. (The only painting he actually signed was the *Mona Lisa*, so there is even dispute as to which paintings were actually done by Leonardo.)[31] His notebooks, on the other hand are filled with sketches — on almost every page of thousands of pages.

---

[31] *Some of his drawings are signed, generally simply as "Leonardo."*

LEONARDO THE ARTIST
(Doing Da Vinci)

"Art is a major path to knowledge."

Student Activity

We looked at a book of paintings from Leonardo da Vinci. I had the students look for similarities and differences in his paintings. How many appeared to be for religious patrons and how many appeared not to be? We also compared them to paintings from just before and soon after his time period. Again – similarities and differences?

For those who considered themselves to be artistic enough, I encouraged them to make their own sketches (the precursor to Leonardo's paintings). For the others, I gave them a couple of pictures from Dover Publications to color.

Leonardo - Renaissance Artist

A	N	D	R	E	A	D	E	L	V	E	R	R	O	C	C	H	I	O	Q
Z	F	I	L	I	P	P	O	B	R	U	N	E	L	L	E	S	C	H	I
Y	U	U	B	X	X	D	S	O	S	P	J	Q	S	U	Q	F	V	W	I
M	N	R	E	F	N	O	C	L	Y	E	O	B	D	L	Z	D	P	E	E
O	F	O	C	E	N	S	L	U	V	U	H	R	H	P	J	J	G	X	V
N	I	F	U	H	E	I	X	V	O	O	L	C	T	T	R	Y	T	N	I
A	N	T	Z	R	I	H	G	W	U	A	L	K	T	R	V	Z	V	L	T
L	I	G	F	O	D	A	U	W	S	V	X	X	K	E	A	S	Y	T	C
I	S	C	S	H	S	J	R	T	W	L	Y	S	T	B	K	I	S	A	E
S	H	I	C	F	O	Y	S	O	Q	G	Y	H	G	S	A	S	T	Z	P
A	E	O	A	P	U	U	B	K	S	O	D	E	V	X	M	H	G	S	S
Q	D	K	I	T	P	M	J	Q	P	C	Q	B	X	Z	F	L	P	Q	R
B	U	K	Y	P	B	Z	A	F	Q	I	U	V	G	A	R	K	U	W	E
A	Z	P	E	E	L	Z	Y	T	G	Y	G	R	X	H	G	N	U	T	P
U	H	R	S	O	B	T	R	X	O	I	B	T	O	Z	H	V	O	J	G
B	G	N	I	T	N	I	A	P	N	O	E	S	I	T	A	E	R	T	V

1. Chiarosuro
2. Unfinished
3. Portraits
4. Treatise on Painting
5. Sfumato
6. Cartoons
7. Sketches
8. Fresco
9. Mona Lisa
10. Renaissance
11. Last Supper
12. Artist

Milan Years – Overview

When Leonardo was ready to move on from Florence, looking for a new job, he wrote Ludovico Sforza, the Duke of Milan [32] an extensive letter requesting a job with him. The timing of the move was surprising, since, Leonardo had just received several big painting contracts in Florence. Because of that, some historians believe Leonardo was actually sent to Milan by the Duke of Florence, as a good-will gesture, rather than going of his own accord.

When Leonardo presented himself to the Duke, he took him a gift of a silver lyre that he had made in the shape of a horse's head.

The Duke's Castle, as it looks today.

This was an amazingly busy time in Leonardo's life. In addition to all he did for the Duke, Leonardo started his notebooks, worked on his music, painted *The Last Supper*, and designed an equestrian monument. Leonardo may have also studied in Pavia for a number of months during this time period, examining both mathematics and science closely there.

In 1485 and 1486 plagues devastated Milan, killing thousands. In the aftermath, Leonardo collaborated with Duke Ludovico to rebuild the city. His plans included ideas for a system of water flowing through the city to improve sanitation. [33] He also drew plans for two sets of streets, one for "vehicles" and one for pedestrians. Locks were built in Milan in 1497 according to his plans.

When Milan fell to French troops, Duke Ludovico fled, and Leonardo da Vinci and his new friend, the mathematician Luca Pacioli, left together, and traveled together to Mantua, and then on to Venice.

---

[32] *Milan was also a fairly powerful city-state in northern Italy.*
[33] *Actually a good idea, but never put into effect.*

Milan Years - Leonardo and the Duke

"If you want to build an armada for the sea, employ these ships to ram in the enemy's ships...."

When Leonardo wrote Ludovico Sforza, the Duke of Milan [34], his extensive letter, it was as if what Leonardo *wanted* to do was more important in his own mind than what he had already done. In spite of all Leonardo's abilities, the Duke most likely hired him to build a statue to the Duke's father. (But more on that later.) The text of Leonardo's letter, his "resume," to the Duke, follows:

To My Lord the Duke of Milan,
Florence, 1482

Most Illustrious Lord,

Having until now sufficiently considered the specimens of all those who proclaim themselves skilled contrivers of instruments of war and that the invention and operation of the said instruments are nothing different to those in common use: I shall endeavor, without prejudice to anyone else, to explain myself to your Excellency showing your Lordship my secrets, and then offering them to your best pleasure and approbation to work with effect at opportune moments as well as all those things which in part, shall be briefly noted below:

---

[34] *Milan was also a fairly powerful "city-state" in northern Italy, ruled by a Duke.*

1. *I have a sort of extremely light and strong bridges, adapted to be most easily carried, and with them you may pursue, and at any time flee from the enemy; and others, secure and indestructible by fire and battle, easy and convenient to lift and place. Also methods to burn and destroy those of the enemy.*

2. *I know how, when a place is besieged, to take the water out of the trenches, and make endless variety of bridges, and covered ways and ladders, and other machines pertaining to such expeditions.*

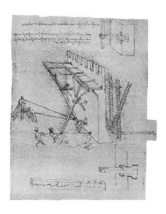

3. *Item, If by reason of the height of the banks, or the strength of the place and its position, it is impossible, when besieging a place, to avail oneself of the plan of bombardment, I have methods for destroying every rock or other fortress, even if it were founded on a rock, etc.*

4. *Again, I have kinds of mortars; most convenient and easy to carry; and with these can fling small stones almost resembling a storm; and with the smoke of these causing great terror to the enemy, to his great detriment and confusion.*

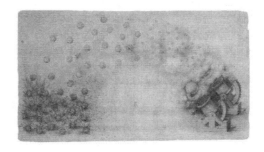

5. *And when the fight should be at sea I have kinds of many machines most efficient for offence and defense; and vessels which will resist the attack of the largest guns and powder and fumes.*

6. *Item, I have means by secret and tortuous mines and ways, made without noise to reach a designated spot, even if it were need to pass under a trench or a river.*

7. *I will make covered chariots, safe and unattackable which, entering among the enemy with their artillery, there is no body of men so great but they would break them. And behind these, infantry could follow quite unhurt and without any hindrance.*

8. *In case of need I will make big guns, mortars and light ordinance of fine and useful forms, out of the common type.*

9. *Where the operation of bombardment should fail, I would contrive catapults…and other machines of marvelous efficacy and not in common use. And in short, according to the variety of cases, I can contrive various and endless means of offence and defense.*

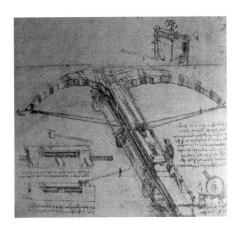

10. *In time of peace I believe I can carry out sculpture in marble, bronze, or clay, and also in painting whatever may be done, and as well as any other, be he whom he may.*

Again the bronze horse may be taken in hand, which is to be to the immortal glory and eternal honour of the prince your father of happy memory, and of the illustrious house of Sforza.

And if any one of the above-named things seem to anyone to be impossible or not feasible, I am most ready to make the experiment in your park, or in whatever place may please your Excellency – to whom I commend myself with the utmost humility.

Leonardo da Vinci

Since war was always a concern for the Duke, Leonardo emphasized his ideas for offensive and defensive war machines more than his artistic abilities.[35] The Duke didn't actually answer Leonardo's letter, but Leonardo moved to Milan the next year, when he was about thirty-years-old, and there received the title of "painter and engineer of the duke."

Leonardo's first job in Milan was to paint a church altarpiece[36]– which he painted completely contrary to the contract he had signed with the monks. He showed Mary with Jesus and his cousin John as babies. But, the altarpiece was very beautiful and very popular. In all, Leonardo would only complete about six paintings during his lengthy stay in Milan, though his students undoubtedly completed others.

The Duke kept Leonardo busy after that, working on a heating system; painting portraits; making cannons and other weapons; building canals; and planning and designing pageants and entertainments for special occasions.

One of the rooms in the Duke's castle — which Leonardo decorated with trees that seem to grow out of the walls.

Leonardo also got very serious about his science studies during his years in Milan, and began recording copious notes in his notebooks.

---

[35] *Even though, throughout his life, Leonardo professed a hatred of war, and the casualties it causes.*
[36] *Altarpieces were the decorative art (usually Bible scenes) behind the altar in churches — and were often quite fancy in those days.*

Milan Years - Leonardo, the Musician

"These two flutes do not change their tone by leaps as most wind instruments do, but in the manner of the human voice."

Like so much else he did, music seemed almost a passing interest for Leonardo da Vinci. But he was reputed to be quite an accomplished musician. Leonardo was fond of singing, and liked to accompany himself with a lute or a lyre.[37] He was well-known during his life for his "impromptu" performances for his friends, and very little of his music was recorded in his notebooks. Leonardo was fascinated by drums, bells, and organ pipes. When he worked on designs for churches, acoustics were a special concern.

Leonardo spent much of his "inventing" time trying to perfect existing musical instruments, as well as trying to develop new ones. He combined his anatomy studies with his musical understanding to develop instruments that worked properly with the limitations of human finger movement and the voice box.

There are some legends circulating that Leonardo invented the violin, which is quite similar to the lyre he liked to play. It's unlikely that he invented it,[38] though he may have contributed in a limited way to its design. He also had designs for an instrument that resembled an early piano.

---

[37] *Also referred to as a "lira" or "lira de braccio."*
[38] *Since most historians date the violin's history back to several decades after his death.*

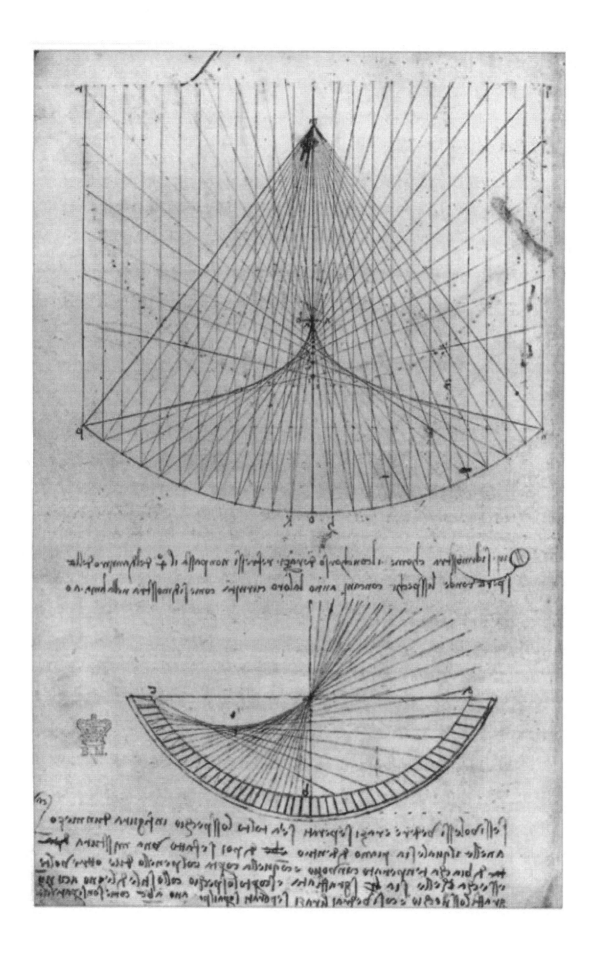

Milan Years - Leonardo, the Mathematician

One of Leonardo's patrons complained: "He is so much distracted from painting by his mathematical experiments as to become intolerant of the brush."

In 1482, Euclid's geometry book *Elements* became available in printed form in Latin.[39] After almost 1,800 years of neglect, interest in geometry was slowly being revitalized.[40] Leonardo taught himself Latin as an adult, so that he could better read classics such as this.

Leonardo met Luca Pacioli, a traveling monk, when they were both working in Milan for the Duke. When Pacioli wrote his own study of mathematics, *De divina proportione* ("*On Divine Proportion*"), he asked Leonardo to provide sixty illustrations for it, as well as some mathematical assistance. Later when Leonardo began designing his famous horse statue (more about that later!) Pacioli helped him with the mathematical problems he faced.

In Leonardo's mind, mathematics went hand in hand with both art and science, and could not really be separated totally from either of them. But for a time, Leonardo was more focused on his mathematical studies than he was on his painting.

---

[39] *Euclid had written Elements in Greek almost 1800 years earlier.*
[40] *Modern geometry "officially" began over one hundred years after Leonardo, in the early 1600's, but interest in the subject was slowly being rekindled in his day.*

LEONARDO DA VINCI AND MATHEMATICS

(Doing Da Vinci)

"Let no man who is not a Mathematician read the elements of my work."

"Mechanics are the paradise of mathematical science, because here we come to the fruit of mathematics."

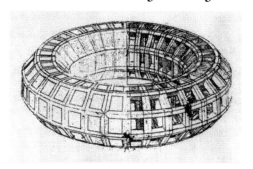

Student Activities

We started by discussing what made da Vinci so interested in Math…What did he do with it? How did he connect it to Art? Could the students come up with their own art/math connections?

With some of the older students we also talked about Golden Ratios and Fibonacci Numbers.[41]

---

[41] *Wikipedia has articles on Golden Ratios and Fibonacci Numbers…I would recommend starting with the one of Fibonacci Numbers, it connects the two concepts, and is more readable by "non-mathematicians."*

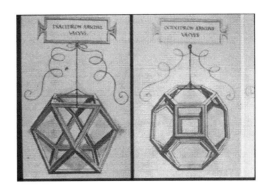

Euclid first wrote his thirteen book geometry series *Elements* in Greek in about 300 B.C. In 1482, with the new printed press, it became the first printed mathematics book – and was now readily available in Latin. Da Vinci taught himself Latin as an adult, so that he could better read classics such as this. While it would be another one hundred years before modern geometry would really come about, in da Vinci's day interest was slowly being rekindled.

Leonardo met Luca Pacioli, a traveling monk about that same time. When Leonardo began designing his famous horse statue, Pacioli helped him with the mathematical problems he faced.

When Pacioli republished his geometry treatise, *De Divina Proportione* ("*On Divine Proportion*") in 1509, it was complete with sixty illustrations by Leonardo da Vinci's (the first of Leonardo's works to ever be published).

In Leonardo's mind, mathematics went hand in hand with both art and science, and could not really be separated totally from either of them. But for a time, Leonardo was more focused on his mathematics studies than he was on his painting.

> *"The elements of mathematics, that is to say number and measure, termed arithmetic and geometry, discourse with supreme truth on discontinuous and continuous quantities. Here no one argues that twice three makes more or less than six, nor that a triangle has angles smaller than two right angles, but with eternal silence, every dissension is destroyed, and in tranquility these sciences are relished by their devotees."*

> *"The other proof which Plato gave to those of Delos is not geometry, because you proceed by the instrument of compasses and ruler, and experience shows it to us. But this is an occupation of the mind and as a consequence, geometry."*

> *The night of St. Andrew's day, I came to the end of the squaring of the circle and it was the end of the night and of the paper on which I was writing. It was concluded at the end of the hour.*

So we should not be surprised to learn that one of Leonardo's patrons complained: "He is so much distracted from painting by his mathematical experiments as to become intolerant of the brush."

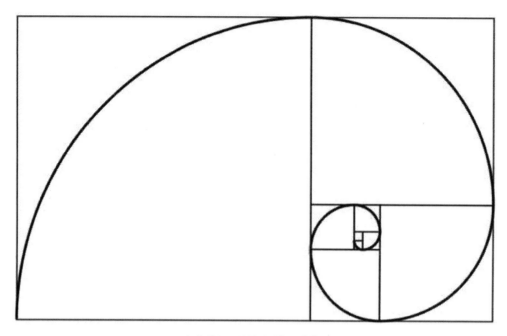

A Fibonacci Spiral

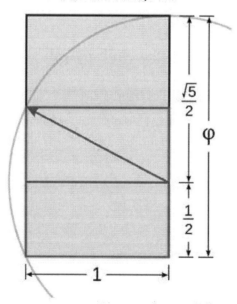

Golden Ratios are used to make Golden Rectangles.

Milan Years - Leonardo, the Scientist

"From science is born creative action,
which is of much more value."

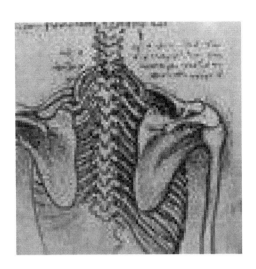

Leonardo da Vinci is considered by many to be the first modern scientist. In his mind and actions, art and science were intimately connected. He used art to improve his science studies, and science to improve his art. He conducted experiments to confirm the observations he made.

He:
- Observed
- Questioned
- Made hypotheses
- Experimented
- Measured
    Humidity
    Altitude
    Distance traveled
    Speed of wind
    Motion of water
    Intensity of Light

Scientific Topics Leonardo studied included:

- Anatomy
    As he learned more about the human body, Leonardo wrote: *"A wonderful instrument, the invention of the supreme master."*

- Astronomy
    "I say that as the moon has no light in itself and yet is luminous, it is inevitable but that its light is caused by some other body."

- Botany
    "A leaf always turns its upper side towards the sky so that it may better receive, on all its surface, the dew which drops gently from the atmosphere."

- Creation vs. Evolution[42]
    "Why do we find the bones of great fishes and oysters and corals and various other shells and sea-snails on the high summits of mountains by the sea, just as we find them in low seas?"

- Geology
    "Mountains are made by the currents of rivers. Mountains are destroyed by the currents of rivers.

- Mechanics
    "Mechanics are the paradise of mathematical science, because here we come to the fruit of mathematics."

- Optics
    "When both eyes direct the pyramid of sight to an object, that object becomes clearly seen and comprehended by the eyes."

- Zoology
    "The smallest feline is a masterpiece."

- and much more…

Leonardo's understanding of optics led him to improvements in shadows and perspective in painting, and his knowledge of geology and geography improved the quality of the landscapes he drew and painted. And his knowledge of anatomy improved the realism in the human figures he drew and painted.

---

[42] *Leonardo didn't believe in Creation, or even "the great flood," but he constantly struggled to get his observations to match his beliefs.*

Milan Years - Leonardo's Notebooks

"He labored much more by his word than in fact or deed."[43]

--Vasari

Leonardo made a practice of always carrying a small notebook with him and then copying his notes, sketches, etc. onto larger sheets each evening.

Leonardo's notebooks were unique for many reasons: In his notebooks, the words typically accompanied the pictures, instead of vice versa. He started his notes on the "back page." He wrote backwards, possibly because he was left-handed and could avoid smearing his ink if he wrote from right to left across the page; or possibly to keep his work "secret," or at least make it harder to read.[44] Leonardo used no punctuation in his notebooks; sometimes he wrote in code and/or shorthand; and he often ran words together. He also wrote some of his notes in Italian and some in Latin after he started learning that language. Needless to say, deciphering his notebooks has been an arduous task!

Leonardo's notebooks were generally unorganized, usually consisting of loose pages, that he only occasionally bound himself. They contained notes about four major categories: anatomy, architecture, mechanics, and painting. His notebooks also included:

- Drafts of letters
- Maps he had drawn
- Menus from what he had eaten recently
- Nature observations
- Notes from borrowed books
- Sketches
- Water
- Weapons

(see page 19 for a longer list)

---

[43] *In the early biography of Leonardo da Vinci by Giorgio Vasari.*

[44] *I personally lean towards the first reason. Writing backwards was probably more efficient for his left handed style, and that's what was important to Leonardo! He was capable of writing "correctly" — he just didn't do it often.*

A number of comprehensive studies were printed in Leonardo's lifetime on architecture and painting. Leonardo had big plans to publish his own notes as early as 1498, and several times after that, as a sort of "encyclopedia" of many subjects, but unfortunately he died before he ever finished that project. He willed his notebooks to one of his students who didn't get them published either. When his student died, the notebooks were forgotten, and over the years they were divided up, sold, stored, and some were even destroyed. For almost three centuries the notebooks were basically lost and/or forgotten, keeping Leonardo da Vinci from being considered the "first" in many scientific endeavors.

More than 7,000 pages from Leonardo's notebooks have been recovered.[45] No other artist or scientist, before or since, has left the kind of "paper trail" that Leonardo da Vinci left – his notebooks were like his journal, sketchbook, scrapbook, and log book, all rolled into one.

Pages from notebookshave been found in obscure places throughout Europe, some even recently, and now the collections mostly reside in major museums in England, Spain, Italy, and France, though some are also in private hands.[46]

His notebook pages have been gathered into at least ten different "major" collections, such as the Codex Arundel, Codex Atlanticus, Codex Trivulianus, and at least forty "minor" ones.

The pages in these collections range in size from 3" x 4" to 8.5" x 12"[47], and each set has anywhere from one page to 238 pages. The notebooks are probably dated between 1473 and 1516, though the exact dates of many of them are not known. Most of the collections have been bound in "modern times"; bound in leather, parchment, or cardboard.

---

[45] *It is believed that there were at least 14,000 pages originally.*
[46] *Bill Gates bought one of the collections in 1995.*
[47] *Between 7x9 centimeters, and 22x29 centimeters.*

Leonardo's Notebooks

R	S	A	E	A	A	F	Y	H	L	N	R	H	S	M	Y	N	H	A
U	Q	I	F	N	T	G	A	C	H	Q	A	F	R	P	H	J	P	U
S	Z	N	N	Y	O	X	B	A	G	V	B	U	Y	J	N	I	S	I
T	A	N	K	L	Y	O	I	C	E	E	G	T	W	A	T	E	R	N
H	Z	J	O	M	T	F	W	Q	O	R	E	N	Y	K	H	G	E	V
G	L	E	Y	A	P	E	Z	U	G	P	W	T	E	S	W	R	T	E
I	G	K	N	Z	A	L	D	Z	R	A	O	P	K	D	X	M	T	N
E	B	Y	S	P	O	U	O	U	A	Q	Z	B	H	K	B	V	E	T
W	J	S	O	E	Y	O	X	S	P	P	I	M	M	F	A	V	L	I
H	M	N	K	J	H	M	K	J	H	S	B	J	R	J	Y	G	F	O
T	S	N	L	O	T	C	O	Y	Y	A	P	D	C	X	J	S	O	N
I	N	W	O	Y	O	I	T	N	P	A	V	A	X	N	U	R	S	P
W	T	T	E	T	E	B	H	E	O	Q	N	H	M	N	M	O	T	L
K	P	X	L	N	E	L	E	O	K	R	A	I	E	P	Q	R	F	A
O	X	L	O	T	M	S	I	T	F	S	T	M	Z	J	K	Z	A	N
W	L	I	S	T	S	O	F	B	O	O	K	S	Z	U	C	L	R	S
L	A	N	V	H	V	P	N	X	B	N	T	T	A	F	N	Q	D	R

1.Menus
2.Sketches
3.Geography
4.Botany
5.Drafts of Letters
6.Geology
7.Lists of Books
8.Maps
9.Weapons
10.Astronomy
11.Invention Plans
12.Notes

Leonardo's "Inventions"

J	P	Q	S	I	T	N	E	Y	E	G	L	A	S	S	E	S
L	K	A	U	T	X	S	Y	I	L	F	T	H	H	M	M	Z
W	Y	O	D	O	X	U	H	E	V	U	D	R	Q	E	T	S
K	W	O	H	D	I	M	E	J	G	P	H	F	C	Y	E	G
A	E	V	I	P	L	H	J	F	L	R	U	H	A	S	W	I
I	R	O	A	H	W	E	B	M	A	I	A	Z	N	Y	C	A
Y	C	W	F	R	U	M	B	S	U	N	Y	E	L	E	O	N
D	S	N	E	D	M	Q	R	O	I	B	L	U	T	P	B	T
H	L	T	S	S	O	L	V	C	A	T	Z	J	L	O	I	C
N	A	W	U	Y	A	Q	A	V	C	T	F	L	V	C	C	R
W	I	W	H	E	E	L	B	A	R	R	O	W	H	S	Y	O
Z	R	U	D	S	D	E	T	J	J	B	Z	K	W	E	C	S
C	E	P	T	R	U	N	U	K	A	B	Y	F	Y	L	L	S
I	A	G	U	G	O	Z	D	N	P	Y	Q	Z	S	E	E	B
K	D	M	C	C	N	R	J	N	K	S	K	G	R	T	Q	O
O	D	S	P	I	N	N	I	N	G	W	H	E	E	L	E	W

1. Bicycle
2. Paddleboat
3. Water Wheel
4. Contact Lenses
5. Giant Crossbow
6. Mechanical Drum
7. Wheelbarrow
8. Spinning Wheel
9. Eye Glasses
10. Aerial Screw
11. Telescope

Milan Years - Leonardo, the Engineer and Inventor

"The perseverance to pursue it and to invent such things…is found in few people."

Many of Leonardo's "inventions" never went beyond the planning stage, often because he was "ahead of his time." Centuries later, many of his ideas were actually built: the helicopter, the tank, the machine gun, the parachute, the bicycle, the wheelbarrow – all existed in Leonardo's mind and notebooks long before they came to be. Our family has a book on the history of tanks. Leonardo's "tank," shown above, is shown first in that historical reference.

One hundred years before Galileo used a telescope to look at the stars, Leonardo was considering the possibility of "making glasses with which…to view the moon at an enlarged size."

Leonardo wanted to save people time with many of his inventions – and he used all of the common "helpers" of his day – screws, pulleys, fly wheels, and springs. Many of these he used in new and unusual ways, and often in plans that went beyond the materials available in his day. A museum near his birthplace has 3-D models of fifty-five of Leonardo's "inventions" and machines.

His plans were varied, including a wide variety of ideas:
- o Aerial Screw
- o Clock
- o Diving Bell
- o Machine Gun
- o Mechanical Drum
- o Naval Cannon
- o Screw-thread Cutter

(see larger list on page 20)

Leonardo worked with water (an especially important commodity in his day) – designing water towers, and canals and locks. We can go today to see locks and canals that Leonardo sketched out and planned centuries ago, and even in our own time and area, we can enjoy the benefit of these "far-fetched" ideas of a forward-looking Leonardo da Vinci.

(Doing Da Vinci)

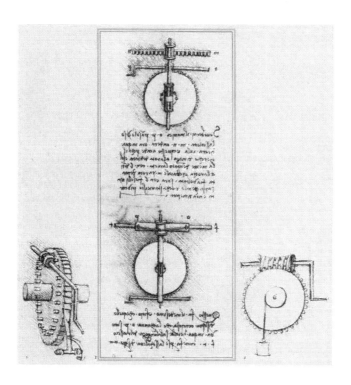

"I have been impressed with the urgency of doing. Knowing is not enough; we must apply. Being willing is not enough; we must do."

Student Activity

The assignment was to figure out a problem that needed to be solved and design a machine using at least one of the following: wheels, pulleys, gears, screws, or levers.

After sketching creative and interesting ideas, we worked on our own designs/models of the different inventions using various amounts of cardboard, cardboard rolls, craft sticks, straws, paper clips, coffee filters, foil sheets, old CDs, computer paper, yarn, rubber bands, and tape.

Leonardo da Vinci was a great artist – but he was also a great scientist and inventor. In fact, he could be rightly called the first modern-day scientist. He was always investigating the world around him – and looking for ways to make things work better. He studied the machines already being used, and constantly sought to understand them. He was one of the first to study friction and its effect on machines.

As most are now, his machines were comprised of various combinations of:
⇒ wheels and axles
⇒ pulleys
⇒ wedges
⇒ screws
⇒ levers
⇒ gears
⇒ springs

He used many of these in new and unusual ways, and often in plans that went beyond the materials available in his day. Leonardo was always looking for new ways to combine these into new machines. He wanted to save people time with many of his inventions. He designed and sometimes even made flying machines, war machines, water machines, and work machines.

A museum near his birthplace has 3-D models of fifty-five of Leonardo's "inventions" and machines, and we saw a traveling exhibit in Huntsville, Alabama that had models of sixteen of his inventions.

Many of Leonardo's "inventions" never went beyond the planning stage during his lifetime, often because he was "ahead of his time." Centuries later, though, many of his ideas were actually built: the helicopter, the tank, the machine gun, the parachute, the bicycle, the wheelbarrow – all existed in Leonardo's mind and notebooks long before they came to be. In fact, one hundred years before Galileo used a telescope to look at the stars, Leonardo was considering the possibility of "making glasses with which…to view the moon at an enlarged size." And because of his skills as an artist, his detailed sketches often showed his ideas very clearly.

A Specific Invention – A Mint Machine:

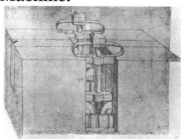

Leonardo da Vinci moved to Rome under the patronage of Giuliano de Medici, brother of Pope Leo X. While there, Leonardo designed a machine for the Pope to mint coins. Banking and coin minting had almost disappeared completely in Europe during the Middle Ages; at the time of the Renaissance, both were slowly coming back.

Surprisingly, the invention of the printing press led first to advancements in minting coins, rather than printing bills. Leonardo used the same principles from the printing press (which had borrowed ideas from grape presses) to develop his machine to mill coins – a method that led to greater uniformity in size and weight.[48]

Of his mint at Rome, Leonardo said, *"It can also be made without a spring. But the screw above must always be joined to the part of the movable sheath…all the coins should be a perfect circle."*

A Specific Idea – a "Robot":

One of the things Leonardo tried to invent was a "robot." Of course, Leonardo didn't call his mechanical man a "robot" – that word wouldn't come into usage until 1921, when humanoid robots would appear in a science fiction play, and decades more would pass before one would actually be built.

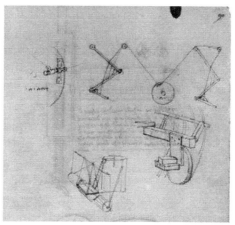

The plans for a humanoid robot in Leonardo's notebooks are dated as early as 1495, making it very probably the first humanoid robot ever designed. There's no proof that Leonardo ever built the robot, though some people argue that he did – but one was built recently, based on his plans.

---

[48] *Milled coins also made it more difficult to "shave" the edges of coins.*

Other Ideas:

What do you think of when you see the following machines that Leonardo designed? Do you think they would work? Do you think we've done anything similar since he drew these? Can you find how Leonardo used pulleys, screws, wheels, and gears in these designs?

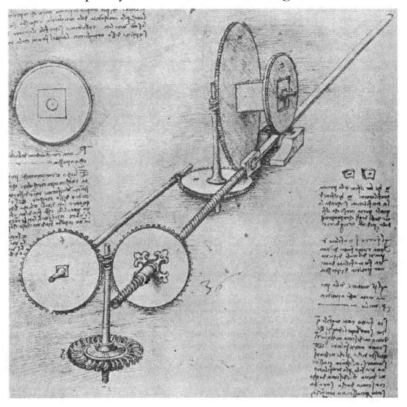

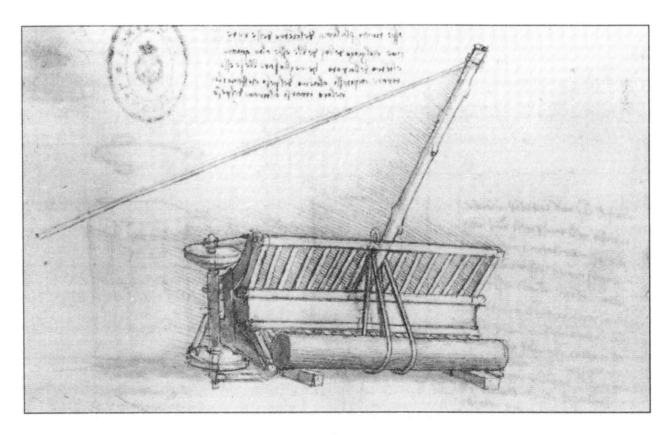

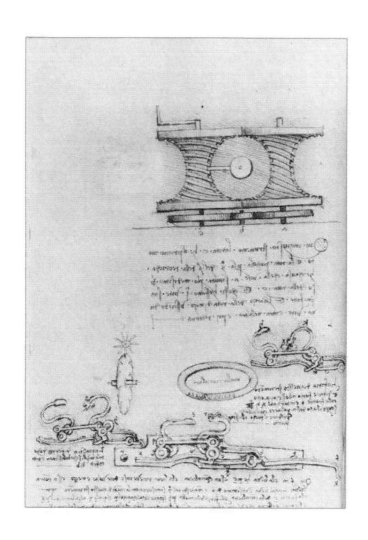

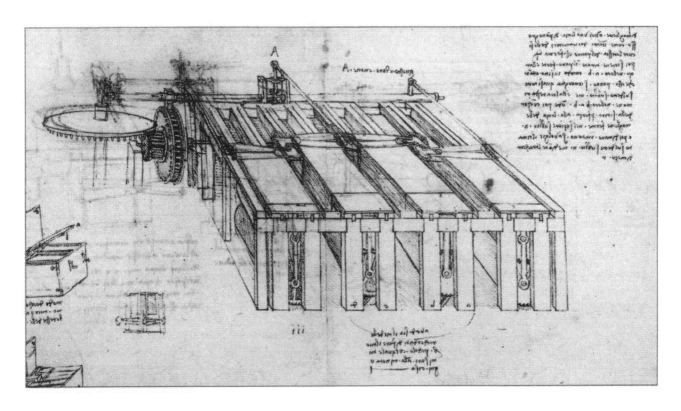

Milan Years - Leonardo's Horse

"Of the horse, I shall say nothing because I know the times."

Duke Galeazzo Sforza had inherited the dukedom of Milan upon his father's death. The idea of a statue to honor his father, the man responsible for bringing Milan its independence, had gnawed at him for some time. After Galeazzo's murder, power passed to Galeazzo's young son, and then quickly to Galeazzo's brother, Ludovico. Ludovico liked the idea of a monument as well – a horse with a rider on its back representing their father, the soldier-hero.

In fact, Ludovico may have hired Leonardo specifically thinking of this project. When Leonardo wrote Ludovico his extensive letter/resume, it was as if what Leonardo *wanted* to do was more important in his own mind than what he had already done. And Leonardo mentioned the horse project almost in passing at the end of his letter to the duke.

Leonardo had some experience in this area; he had helped his master, Andrea del Verrocchio, in his research for an equestrian statue. (Verrocchio in Venice in 1488, and Donatello in Padua in 1453, had both completed equestrian monuments to military heroes, both of which Leonardo would have been familiar with.)

Donatello's Monument in Padua

93

The Duke never answered Leonardo's letter, but Leonardo moved to Milan the next year, when he was about thirty-years-old, and there received the title of "painter and engineer of the duke." The Duke most likely hired him specifically to build the statue which da Vinci eventually worked in among his other projects. It was an interesting assignment for Leonardo to even contemplate –he considered sculpting to be much inferior to painting!

Original plans called for the statue to be life-size, with the horse in a rearing position. It was an interesting project for Leonardo to even contemplate – considering his attitude toward sculpting.[49]

While working on *The Last Supper*, Leonardo would also work on his horse sculpture. As with his other projects, Leonardo could not be rushed. He spent years studying horses, even dissecting a few to make sure he understood how their muscles worked together.

He also spent years on the design for the monument, visiting many other similar statues in the area. His had to be better than all the others! Of course, by 1485, three years after hiring Leonardo, the Duke was getting impatient to have his monument completed, and by 1489 he was actually looking for another artist to take over the project.

It didn't help that over time, the Duke also changed his mind about what he wanted: He decided his statue should be four times life-size, which would make it the largest monument of its kind in that day. The horse was now to be twenty-four feet tall. To accommodate the larger size, Leonardo had to change the positioning of the horse from rearing to standing. He also worked hard to develop a new system for casting the statue, so it could be cast in one piece.[50] Leonardo did not want to use the current system of "lost wax" casting, which caused a number of problems, including that the mold was never reusable in this method.[51] He invented a new way to use a double mold to make the cast.[52] And he planned to cast the horse upside down, to resolve some of the problems with the weight in a statue of this size.

By 1493, just in time for the wedding of Bianca Sforza, daughter of the Duke of Milan, and Emperor Maximilian, Leonardo unveiled a twenty-four feet tall clay model of the horse. It was beautiful, and people came from miles away to gaze at it. In 1494 he finally began preparing the molds for the actual statue.

The amount of metal needed to cast was tremendous, approximately eighty tons, and Leonardo worked to collect it while he "perfected" his design and technique. Unfortunately,

---

[49] *Leonardo considered sculpting to be much inferior to painting!*

[50] *Something that had never been done for a statue of this size.*

[51] *In the "lost-wax" method, a model was made out of wax, the mold would be made over the wax – and then the wax was melted out and replaced with bronze.*

[52] *In 1699 someone would finally try Leonardo's double mold method. It worked, and a statue of King Louis XIV was made with it – which lasted almost one hundred years until it was destroyed during the French Revolution.*

Milan was attacked by France in 1499 and had to use the dedicated metal for cannon balls.

Leonardo was quoted as saying at that time, "Of the horse I shall say nothing because I know the times."

Milan still lost the battle with the French, the Duke fled, and so did Leonardo. The French archers used his huge clay horse for target practice, and it eventually crumbled into nothing.

In 1508 Leonardo would be invited to make a statue for the Italian general, Trivulzio, who had led the French troops against Milan. Leonardo actually worked on plans for it, but that statue was never completed either.

Leonardo would lament the unfinished horse for the rest of his life: *"Of the horse, I shall say nothing, because I know the times."*

* * * * *

In 1966, 467 years after the French invasion halted the equine project, sketches of Leonardo da Vinci's horse were rediscovered in Spain. And in 1977 *National Geographic* ran a very short piece about "The Horse That Never Was." Charles Dent, a United Airlines pilot, read the article, and became very interested in finally building Leonardo's horse as a gift to Italy.

Over the next seventeen years, Charles Dent raised money, had a special dome built to work in, studied horses, came up with an initial design and got the first life size model of the horse completed.[53] In 1994, he died, before the work had been completed. His foundation, *Leonardo da Vinci's Horse, Inc.*, continued, and in 1996 the first attempt at an enlarged model failed. Something would have to be done differently with the eight foot model, and a new sculptor, Nina Akamu, was hired to finish work on *The Horse*. In 1998, Akamu's new eight foot model was completed, followed quickly by a twenty-four-foot clay model. Work was progressing.

On September 10, 1999, exactly five hundred years after the soldiers had destroyed Leonardo's clay model, Charles Dent and Leonardo da Vinci's dream horse was unveiled in Milan Italy.[54] Nina Akamu had completed their project. *The Horse* stands proudly there on a marble pedestal.[55]

---

[53] *He decided to do just a horse, without a rider.*

[54] *Total costs for the project exceeded $4 million.*

[55] *Jean Fritz wrote a great children's book, Leonardo's Horse, about both Leonardo's work on the horse, and Dent's project almost 500 years later.*

The horse and models of some of the portions of the mold – on display in Milan.

In October 1999 one more casting was made from the mold, this time for *The American Horse*, which now stands proudly at the Frederik Meijer Gardens in Grand Rapids, Michigan. This horse stands on the ground, rather than on a pedestal, so that visitors can walk right up to it.

In the year 2,000, a fifteen inch scale model of Leonardo's horse was given to the people of Milan to go with *Leonardo's Horse*. It is known as "the Horse for the Blind" – a miniature that can be "seen" by the blind, by touching it. In November 2001, an eight-foot replica of *Leonardo's Horse* was donated to Leonardo's home town.

With the help of many others, Da Vinci's promise to the Duke had finally been fulfilled:

> *"In time of peace I believe I can carry out sculpture in marble, bronze, or clay, and also in painting whatever may be done, and as well as any other, be he whom he may... Again the bronze horse may be taken in hand, which is to be to the immortal glory and eternal honour of the prince your father of happy memory..."*

And so, Leonardo's "Horse That Never Was" finally *is*, in multiple places!

Da Vinci's Horse was also in Atlanta, Georgia for a time.

(Doing Da Vinci)

 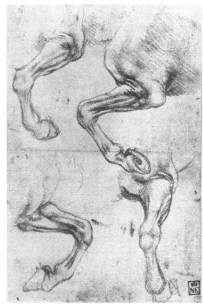

"Again the bronze horse may be taken in hand, which is to be to the immortal glory and eternal honour of the prince your father of happy memory, and of the illustrious house of Sforza."

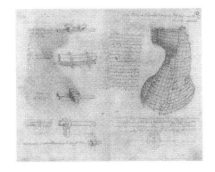

Student Activity

After sketching horses, we worked on our own Horse Sculptures, using modeling clay, toothpicks, pipe cleaners, straws, and popsicle sticks.

Leonardo's Horse

C	J	J	W	C	Q	V	T	I	S	G	A	J	L	A	I	H
A	H	B	N	N	X	E	X	P	C	N	I	P	E	T	E	B
R	K	A	D	I	K	V	E	I	Z	N	K	F	A	W	R	L
D	I	U	R	Y	N	D	T	V	P	S	I	L	T	V	U	D
X	K	J	L	L	E	A	T	S	U	P	Y	V	G	L	T	M
E	T	P	T	S	E	O	A	R	I	H	Q	B	A	G	P	O
S	K	E	T	C	H	S	X	K	E	T	R	E	S	D	L	N
B	M	A	N	K	V	U	D	U	A	O	R	Y	J	S	U	U
E	L	M	I	L	A	N	T	E	N	M	X	A	H	I	C	M
N	A	W	H	I	M	A	Y	Z	N	K	U	C	W	E	S	E
M	P	C	K	R	T	O	E	X	Z	T	N	H	R	E	W	N
M	A	T	L	S	Q	J	L	I	J	E	C	O	L	Z	Z	T
U	O	Y	A	L	C	A	P	D	R	L	U	R	E	X	I	W
U	J	D	D	C	F	D	D	F	J	Y	O	S	F	L	B	O
I	C	L	E	P	S	E	L	C	S	U	M	E	W	R	K	T
M	T	R	Z	L	E	Z	K	R	K	L	U	Q	T	A	J	Z

1.Statue	7.Clay	13.Milan
2.Gift	8.Model	14.Mold
3.Sculpture	9.Charles Dent	15.Nina Akamu
4.Bronze	10.Sketch	16.Italy
5.Muscles	11.Duke	17.Artist
6.Pedestal	12.Monument	18.Da Vinci

Milan Years - *The Last Supper*

"When you wish to represent a man speaking to a number of people, consider the matter of which he has to treat and adapt his action to the subject. Thus if he speaks persuasively, let his action be appropriate to it..."

The following sections are excerpted from the author's small booklet, *Exploring da Vinci's Last Supper.*

"One of You Shall Betray Me."

In the New Testament, the four gospels of Matthew, Mark, Luke and John all mention the moment that Leonardo portrays in his painting of the *Last Supper*, the moment during the Passover meal when Christ alarms his disciples by announcing, "Verily I say unto you, that one of you shall betray me."

Here's how Leonardo chose to portray the event: He put Christ in the center, with a window behind him, giving him the effect of a halo, without actually including one. Christ is the focal point of the picture, with his head and hands making a triangle (often seen as the symbol of perfection, and of the trinity).

Christ's robe is blue and red, which can be seen to indicate his divine side and his earthly side. Even the appearance of his hands coincides with that – the one on the "earthly" side is clenched, as if anticipating his death on the cross, and the one on his left (our right) is open wide, possibly indicating his openness to the sacrifice he is about to give. Christ's mouth is partially open as if he just uttered the words.

Due to the door cut out in the bottom of the Last Supper, we can no longer tell how Leonardo painted Christ's feet, but preparatory drawings show his feet crossed, as they would later be on the cross.

Da Vinci then groups the disciples in groups of three, with each group reacting to the surprise announcement. On Christ's immediate left, James the Elder is drawing back in terror, Thomas is advancing towards Christ with a raised finger, and Philip rises, bending forward, laying his hand on his own chest. Thomas can be seen as asking "Who is the traitor" or "Are you sure?" His raised finger could also represent after Christ has risen, and Doubting Thomas says he won't believe until he has put his finger in the nail wounds.

The second group on Christ's left are conversing with each other. Matthew unites the group, extending his hands towards the Savior. Thaddeus shows surprise, doubt, and suspicion. Simon (the oldest of the disciples) is deep in thought and appears troubled.

To the immediate right of Christ are John, the youngest of the disciples (who bends towards Peter, the eldest of the disciples), Judas (holding the purse with the money he has received for betraying Christ), and Peter grasping the right shoulder of John. Peter is holding a knife that "accidently" touches Judas, as Judas overturns a salt-cellar at the surprising announcement. It looks like Peter is asking John a question that John doesn't know the answer to.

At the other end of the table Bartholomew is standing, bending forward with both his hands on the table, as if he is trying to understand. James the Younger (the most damaged portion of the painting) has his hand on Peter's shoulder, and Andrew appears horrified at the thought of betrayal, and as if he wants to declare himself innocent. His eyes show astonishment and fear.

The History of the Da Vinci's Last Supper
The following is from the Last Supper chapter of the non-fiction work, Da Vinci: His Life and His Legacy.

In 1495, three years after Columbus discovered the New World, Leonardo da Vinci started his *Last Supper* mural for the monks' dining room at the Santa Maria delle Grazie.

(Donato Bramante was working on the dome there at the same time.) The Last Supper was a popular theme for frescos before and since his day, but Leonardo chose to do it in a unique manner – painting the disciples in groups of three at the table, each reacting to Christ's statement, "One of you will betray me." Additionally, he chose to depict "modern day" clothes, foods, and dishes for the picture, instead of those from the New Testament era, so that the monks there could relate better to it.

Even before he could start painting, Leonardo had to do countless sketches in preparation. He wanted each detail to be perfect. He agonized the longest over the faces for Christ and for Judas. One story is that he had to go to the worst part of Milan to find a face horrible enough to use for his model of Judas.

Another legend is that he inadvertently used the same person as his model for both Christ and Judas, a man who had become hardened in the years between the two portions of the picture. Christ and Judas were the last two faces he did so not much time separated the painting of the two of them, and so that story is unlikely. And yet a third legend is that the head monk complained to Leonardo that he was taking too long to finish the painting, and Leonardo offered to use **his** face for the model for Judas…bringing an end to that complaint.

Unfortunately, *The Last Supper* was yet another of Leonardo's experiments, since he didn't like the current way of painting frescos. Fresco painting techniques required an artist to apply wet plaster to a section of a wall, and then paint that section quickly with water-based paints. This method effectively bonded the paint to the plaster – which is why even after centuries, frescoes done this way have vibrant colors.

Leonardo wanted to paint slowly, and to be able to make changes as he went along. He developed a new paint solution of varnish and oil which he could use on a dry wall and change along the way. Because Leonardo was a perfectionist, and was distracted by other projects, he spent many years working on the mural. Sadly, Leonardo had not perfected his new technique, and even in his lifetime the paint of his incredible *Last Supper* mural began to flake off the wall.

In 1652, monks cut a door in the wall where *The Last Supper* is painted, cutting out the feet of Christ in the process. At another point, in 1796, French soldiers under Napoleon staying in the monastery defaced the painting by throwing things at it.

During World War II, the wall was reinforced, and sand bags were placed behind the wall with the painting. A bomb hit the monastery only a few feet away from the wall, fortunately causing no more damage to the painting.

The Last Supper is a masterpiece, and ranks with Leonardo's *Mona Lisa* for the fame associated with it. Even in Leonardo's lifetime, it was appreciated. When the French King, Louis XII, saw the painting, he was so impressed by it – he wanted to take it back to France – wall and all! Obviously not a practical idea, so the painting stayed where it was. All over the world, copies of it hang on home and church walls alike.

Painting the *Last Supper*

*This section is a fictionalized (but very historically accurate)
account of the painting of the Last Supper.
It is excerpted from* Leonardo: Masterpieces in Milan.

Soon after the Duke and Duchess returned from Vigevano, the Duke surprised Leonardo by asking him to paint a mural in the Santa Maria delle Grazie Church. Leonardo was surprised that with all the other tasks the Duke had assigned him, that he would add one more important job to those he was already doing. But the Duke was now paying his salary full-time, as well as that of several of his apprentices, and if that's what the Duke desired, Leonardo would surely do his best to comply.

Leonardo walked over to the church to see the space he would be painting. A large wall, thirty feet across and fourteen feet high, in the Dining Room lay bare, awaiting the touch of the master. Leonardo walked around the room, taking in the wall from numerous angles. "Yes, I will paint the *Last Supper* on that wall. It will be an appropriate picture for the monks to view as they sup here."

As Leonardo contemplated the task, he took out his omnipresent notebook and began to sketch some ideas of how to display Christ and the disciples in the painting. The first few pictures were not to his liking, but then he struck on an idea that did appeal to him. He would capture the moment at which Christ had told the disciples that one of them would betray him. With that decision, the sketches came quicker as he drew out the disciples, huddled in groups of three, as they contemplated the horror of such a thing.

Leonardo quickly decided he would dress the disciples in contemporary clothing, so that the monks could more easily identify with them, rather than in the costumes of Christ's day, as was the tradition with most painters.

Once again, the pressure started almost immediately for Leonardo to begin and then complete the painting quickly. But, for this project, Leonardo would not be rushed, not even for the Duke.

Leonardo abhorred the usual wet plaster method of painting frescoes, since it required working quickly. Most fresco painters combined their paint with plaster, and applied it to the surface quickly, so that the work could be done before the plaster dried.

But Leonardo would not paint anything quickly and therefore refused to use that method. He wanted to be able to paint his mural slowly, to make adjustments as he went along. He had been experimenting with a new method of fresco painting using a mixture of varnish and oil that would allow him to paint that way, and that's the method he planned to employ here.

As Leonardo finished his preliminary drawings of the disciples and the table in from of them, he slowly started to transfer the figures to the wall in the Dining Room. Even when only the cartoon (the drawings) had been done on the wall, people would stop to look in astonishment. Even without paint, it was as if the larger-than-life disciples were speaking and as if one could reach out and touch the Passover food on the table. All were anxious to see the work completed.

But Leonardo would not be rushed. He wanted the colors to be just right. He wanted to make sure the expressions on their faces were perfect. He would not be hurried by anyone, not even an impatient Duke or a set of frustrated monks. They would have to put up with the mess in the Dining Room longer. He had not asked for this assignment, but if he was going to do it, he was going to do it on his timetable, and he was going to do it well.

When Leonardo finally started painting, he began with the table and the table settings, finishing the food and the blue designs on the edges of the white tablecloth last.

He started work on the twelve disciples in the various groupings of three that he planned to display them in. He had pondered how best to show them, and had considered how little he knew about most of them. He had always found Peter to be a fellow of conflicted emotions with his insistence of perfect obedience to Jesus, and yet his denials of him within a week of this dinner. But he particularly liked the story of Peter's attempted defense of the Master in the garden when he cut off the ear of one of the arresting soldiers. And so, Leonardo had found himself drawing a small knife in Peter's hand. It could be seen as part of the meal, intended only for the cutting of the bread they were sharing, but for Leonardo it would hold a double meaning.

Of course, Leonardo knew that Judas would be an especially important part of the painting, and he put him in the same grouping with Peter, turned to look at Jesus. Leonardo wanted the face of Judas to show the anger and betrayal that he must have felt inside, even if no one else there had been aware of it. Leonardo carefully posed him, looking straight at Jesus. Judas would need no dagger in his hand; he had daggers in his eyes. Leonardo had searched the streets of Milan for many months, looking for just the right face to sketch for the model of this disciple.

With Peter and Judas carefully painted, Leonardo considered the color combinations he would use in each of the disciples' robes. He was always very meticulous about his color choices, knowing that the right choices would mean everything in the outcome of his mural. Several other artists had painted the *Last Supper* in subdued colors, as if they wanted the painting to fade into the background of the wall it covered, but not Leonardo. He wanted his colors to be bright and vivid. If he was going to be tasked with such a project as this, all who entered this dining room in the future should be drawn to the painting.

Leonardo mixed the various colored powders he planned to use on the fresco that day. He only planned to paint a small section of one disciple at this point. Even with all the pressure from the monks and the Duke to complete this project sooner rather than later, Leonardo still would not be rushed. Each disciple would be painstakingly painted, as if he was the only person that counted in that group. Only then would Leonardo move on to the next disciple and then on to the next.

Leonardo planned to focus on their torsos first, and come back to the legs and feet that could be seen protruding from under the tablecloth later. He would not need as many colors for the lower portion of the painting, since there he would primarily be painting feet and sandals.

As Leonardo painstakingly applied the paint to the sandals of the disciples, Leonardo tried to remember the Bible stories he had heard somewhere along the way. Had Jesus washed the disciples' feet before or after they had partaken of this meal? He just couldn't remember. But regardless, he thought of that story as he painted the thirteen sets of feet. Feet shod only in sandals would have been dirty feet to wash indeed.

When Leonardo tired of work on the fresco, he would wander outside to watch Donato Bramante's work on the dome…

Leonardo turned back to his art with a vengeance after his mother's death. His appearances at the church where he had been painting the *Last Supper* fresco became more frequent. He could often be found on his scaffolding, tirelessly painting or repainting one small section, and then another.

As he stood in the middle of the room taking in the large painting, he could almost hear the conversations in the little groups of three as they discussed the shocking remarks that Jesus had just made. Now that the people were complete, and his focus had come back, he was ready to finish their surroundings. Leonardo first sketched out the walls surrounding the large table, the two side walls and the back wall in the distance.

Now he climbed up on his scaffolding to draw these backgrounds onto the wall itself. On each side wall he was placing four red-colored tapestries. He had considered making each tapestry unique, but he didn't want to take away from the central figures of the painting, and had decided instead on geometric patterns on each of them. That would give them depth and interest without making them overwhelm the people. Between the tapestries would be doorways leading to the unknown.

Finally, he drew in the windows on the rear wall of the painting. Here he included a small portion of the landscape behind, again not wanting to detract from the people in the painting, but wanting to give the picture completeness.

When the walls had been completely drawn in, Leonardo turned his attention to the ceiling in the picture. He planned to give the ceiling a three-dimensional feel with a simple lattice-work design across the top of the room. Again, it would help complete the setting without competing with the focus.

With the background of the *Last Supper* complete, Leonardo made a few final finishing touches on the painting. He had completed the table portion much earlier, but now he wanted the orange slices and fish to be more vivid. Then Leonardo set down his brushes and stepped back from the project. After so many years of working on it, he was ready to call it finished. Even after all this time with students and apprentices, he normally did his own clean up, but for once he didn't feel like cleaning up after himself. Leonardo took off his work apron, and motioned to his apprentices who had been watching from nearby. They came forward quickly, and started the tedious cleaning process. Meanwhile, Leonardo walked to the far side of the dining room, to take one last look at his work, and walked out of the room...

More Details on the Painting Itself

Leonardo's mural is painted on a wall in the dining hall of the Santa Maria delle Grazie Monastery. The usual method to do murals was to fresco them, but Leonardo tried to paint the wall more like he painted on wood – so that he could make changes to it as he went.

The room is approximately 120 feet by 30 feet. The painting occupies most of the north wall (approximately 30 feet by 15 feet). The painting starts about eight to ten feet above the ground in the dining room. Windows on the left side of the room let in the late day light, lighting up all the faces except that of Judas (which stayed dark).

The figures are about fifty percent larger than life size (and Christ is slightly larger than the rest of the disciples). If standing completely, Leonardo's figures would be nine feet tall. Leonardo used proportion to do such a good job of enlarging the figures as much as he did. He also used perspective to accentuate Christ in the middle of the painting, as well as His size (He is slightly larger than the disciples), and the window behind him (rather than the traditional halo). The hands and faces show the disciples' emotions at Christ's shocking announcement.

The Painting over Time

The monastery was started in 1462, and enlarged in 1490. In 1495 Leonardo da Vinci was assigned to paint the mural at one end of the dining room, and another painter was assigned to fresco the other end at the same time. The fresco across from da Vinci's was done in the Tuscany style, hasn't been preserved at all, and yet today is more vibrant.

Even in Leonardo's lifetime, the painting was starting to deteriorate, and in 1556 Giorgio Vasari, the art historian, referred to the painting as merely a "muddle of blots."

The Last Supper has suffered greatly since then as well. The monks wanted to protect it at one point, and hung a curtain over it, opening it only for special visitors. Unfortunately, the curtain scratched the painting as it went back and forth. In addition, it trapped moisture between the curtain and the wall, causing more damage.

Over the centuries, starting in the 18th century, and then again in the 19th century, many artists have attempted to "restore" *The Last Supper*, often making the situation worse in the process. A major restoration was begun in 1977. An artist, Dr. Pinin Brambilla Barcilon, worked on the mural with a small microscope, removing centuries of dirt and grime, and the extra paint that had been applied since Leonardo's day. Twenty-two years later, she finally finished the project, which unfortunately met with mixed reviews from art critics around the world. Some thought she had gone too far with the removal of the paint, though others thought she had done an incredible job. (Having seen the painting recently, I go with the latter position – she did a remarkable job.)

By 1550 or so, a traveler wrote of the painting that it was "half spoiled"; another spoke of it as "lost" and another as "quite gone." In time, the cracks it increased, and quickly began to run together.

In 1652 a large door into the room was added, destroying the feet of Christ and several of the disciples. Additionally, the hammering and chiseling on the wall to make the door caused more damage to the painting.

Sometime around 1726, Pietro Bellotti, an inferior painter, offered to restore the painting, and proceeded to cover the entire thing with paint…and at other times it was partially touched up with watercolors. By 1770 Giuseppe Mazza had been hired to "fix" the painting. He scraped the painting and prepared to add paint himself, redoing all but three of the heads.

In 1796 Napoleon Bonaparte came through Milan with his army. After visiting the painting, he ordered that no damage be done to it and that the military stay out of the room. But he had no sooner left than another general arrived, breaking open the door and converting the dining room into a stable for the military's horses. (There was more mold damage to the painting as a result.)

Other problems were caused for the painting because the wall it is on is not far from the kitchen…and the convent is not built on a high place in Milan. In 1800 excessive rain caused water in the convent to be more than two feet high, causing serious problems for the painting.

In 1807 Prince Eugene (Beauharnais), the Viceroy of the Kingdom of Italy, ordered that the Last Supper should be repaired and repainted. Windows were added to the room, the dining hall was aired out and dried, and the floor removed. He had a layer of charcoal laid down to repel humidity.

Within the next few years, magistrates succeeded in shutting off the door and walling up the entrance to the dining room. For a time the only way to see the painting was to descend into the room by a ladder from the pulpit.

During World War II, the wall was reinforced, and sand bags were placed behind the wall with the painting. In 1943 Milan was bombed, and a bomb did hit the monastery only a few feet away from the right wall, fortunately causing no more damage to the painting nor to Bramante's dome. (The left side of the chapel was destroyed at that time.)

Today, there is only twenty percent of the original color left in the Last Supper painting.

Copies of da Vinci's Last Supper

Marco da Oggino one of da Vinci's students, made a small copy of da Vinci's mural about 1515 so that he could then make a larger copy on the wall of the convent of Castellazzo.

This copy is sometimes attributed to Oggiono, and sometimes to Giampietrino, another member of Leonardo's studio.

Sometime before 1565 another copy was made in fresco by Pietro Lovino at Ponte Capriasca. One of the changes he made was to put their names under each disciple. And in 1612 Andrea Bianchi (Vespino) was hired by Cardinal Frederick Borromeo to make a full size copy of it, so that it would not be lost forever.

In the late 1700's Raffaello Morghen made an engraving of the Last Supper, though it appears to have been based on Oggino's copy, rather than da Vinci's original.

In 1807 Giuseppe Bossi was ordered by the Viceroy to help make a mosaic copy of Leonardo's mural. He made a full size cartoon after looking at every copy of da Vinci's Last Supper he could find (apparently more than twenty). He mostly referenced the full size copy by Vespino. Once the cartoon was completed Bossi had a piece of canvas prepared and then sketched the entire painting on it. Then Bossi painted the sky/landscape, and then the head of Christ and three of the disciples. Bossi got ill before he could complete the sketch and went back to studying the information available from previous copies and authors of da Vinci's day. When he was done a mosaic was made based on his work, approximately 28 feet long and 18 feet high.

Milan Years - Leonardo's Robot

"I wish to work miracles"[56]

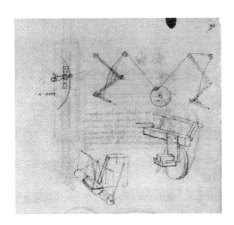

It is thought by some that Leonardo's focus on the measurements and mechanics of the human body came from his desire to build a human-type robot. The Institute and Museum of the History of Science in Florence, Italy recently did a computer analysis of some of Leonardo's drawings, proving that he had indeed made plans for a robot. His robot design included a jaw that opened and closed, a head that moved back and forth, and arms that could wave. His robot was to be dressed as a medieval knight.

Of course, Leonardo didn't call his mechanical man a "robot" – that word wouldn't come into usage until 1921, when humanoid robots would appear in a science fiction play, and decades more would pass before one would actually be built.

The plans for a humanoid robot in Leonardo's notebooks are dated as early as 1495, making it very probably the first humanoid robot ever designed. There's no proof that Leonardo ever built the robot, though some people argue that he did – but one was built recently, based on his plans.

---

[56] *A comment Leonardo made about his anatomy work.*

Final Time in Milan

The following is the first chapter of *Leonardo to Mantua and Beyond*, and describes da Vinci's final days in Milan before his departure:

As the fall weather began cooling off, Leonardo was putting the final touches on his Last Supper mural. The first rumors had reached Milan that King Louis XII of France was on his way, claiming he had hereditary rights and a legitimate claim to the rule of the city. When the rumors intensified, Duke Ludovico called his trusted military engineer to him. When Leonardo appeared in the inner portions of the castle, it was clear that the duke was distraught.

Leonardo stood in front of him, wondering what the latest project might be that Ludovico would want him to turn his attention to and why it was causing him such concern. He had just finished painting the Last Supper mural after all this time, and was sure that the duke must have some other artistic task to fill his hours.

But the duke was not interested in discussing art this time around. The duke called Leonardo closer to him and explained his newest assignment in hushed tones. "It appears that the French troops will be arriving soon. I had hoped to keep them away longer, but the Venetians have convinced them that now is a good time to attack Milan.

"I am planning to leave while I still can, taking some of my closest servants and staff along with me. As my military advisor I would like you to remain behind and assess the situation. I need to know their intentions. Are they just coming in to exhibit a show of force and appease the Venetians? Or do they plan to stay? Will they discuss peaceful options or are they only interested in fighting? And are their weapons as formidable as we've heard?"

Leonardo nodded as he took in all that Ludovico was instructing him. "I understand."

The duke went on, "You should continue your artwork when you can, so that the French are less likely to suspect you of being my advisor. But I would like you to travel through the city as much as possible, and keep your eyes open. You can use the excuse of examining the canals to make sure they are functioning properly. You are one of my canal architects; that should alleviate any suspicions as to why you are traveling through the city so much, instead of just staying in your studio."

Leonardo could hear the concern in the duke's voice, and tried to calm him. "I am sure that I can explain my duties adequately enough to please any that might inquire."

It was obvious that the duke was tired, and Leonardo prepared to depart. The duke leaned forward again. "Please be careful, Leonardo the Florentine. The French have spies throughout the city. You must strive to discover their intentions without being discovered yourself." The duke sat back, dismissing Leonardo with a tired wave.

Leonardo left the hall and headed out of the castle towards the streets of Milan. He wondered again at the strange encounters he had had in and near his favorite bookstore, the snippets of French he had picked up there on multiple occasions, and the surprise from the owner when he had asked for books in French. Could that all have been related to the French troops the duke was now expecting in Milan?

Leonardo made his way across Milan towards the large cathedral in the center of town. The sight of the Duomo reaching into the sky usually cheered him and helped lift his spirits. But now, as he passed the Duomo and walked towards his workshop, he again pondered all that the duke had told him and the variety of things he had overheard. He would certainly do his best to determine what the French might have in mind, though as an avowed pacifist he certainly hoped it would not mean war.

--

Before Leonardo had much time to further investigate the goings on in the city, he received word that Duke Ludovico had indeed fled. Leonardo had been left behind with instructions from the duke to keep him apprised of the situation in Milan. As long as his own safety was not in jeopardy, Leonardo would be his eyes and ears in the city.

Leonardo tried to stay busy at his studio as the French entered Milan, but ignoring their entrance altogether was impossible. Relenting, Leonardo came out to the cobblestone street leading from the main city gate towards the duke's castle. He stood shoulder to shoulder with a variety of other workers who were as curious as he.

He had stepped out just in time to see the French king entering the streets of Milan under a golden, fur-lined canopy. The king was met by a group of Milanese nobility, cardinals, and ambassadors who had come out to the square to welcome him. *It didn't take long for them to change allegiance,* Leonardo thought gravely.

The initial part of the king's procession was followed by a number of princes, each accompanied by one hundred and fifty horsemen. One prince in particular caught Leonardo's attention. He looked as magnificent as the king himself. He and his horsemen were all clothed in velvet, riding horses with gold and silver coverings. The prince had rings on each of his fingers and a white cloak over his shoulders, and he wore a black cap with a white feather and a pearl-embroidered rim over his long dark hair.

As Leonardo wondered who this prince could be, he heard someone in the crowd across from him yell, "Welcome, Duke of Valentinois." *Duke Valentinois?* Leonardo was surprised. In spite of his attempts to avoid politics, he had heard some stories about this new duke, Cesare Borgia—a dangerous man, it was said. He was certainly a man to watch out for.

As the procession continued in front of him, Leonardo was startled to find his good friend Luca Pacioli standing in the crowd next to him. "Leonardo, we must flee the city. There are waves and waves of soldiers coming into the city. Our association with the duke will be discovered and we will not be safe here."

Leonardo turned sadly toward his friend, and then back to the parade in front of them, before answering slowly, "My life is not yet in danger, and I have not accomplished all that the duke would have me to do. I am not willing to run from the French just yet."

Through the next couple of months Leonardo continued to be encouraged to flee the city by others he respected, but he was torn. He certainly didn't want to stay in Milan and have trouble with the French. But surely they would see him as only an artist, so what difficulties could he have? As he contemplated his options, Leonardo sought out one of the few Medici bankers who had not yet fled Milan, and transferred what money he had in savings to a bank in Florence, just in case.

He also packed up some of his most precious books and sketches. He would send them with one of his servants to his uncle's home in Vinci. Uncle Francesco, his father's brother, had been his closest relative growing up, and Leonardo was sure he would willingly take care of Leonardo's possessions while Leonardo determined what might be next in his life.

As the last vestiges of autumn gave way completely to the cold winter of December, Leonardo came to the realization that his options in Milan had run out, some literally. Word arrived that Duke Ludovico had gone into hiding and would not be returning. As many had suspected, the French presence in the city was not going away anytime soon.

Nevertheless, when Luca came to encourage his departure one last time before he set out with just his own servant, it was with great reluctance that Leonardo consented, gathering a few things from his studio. He realized as he packed that he was taking even less out of Milan than he had brought into the city seventeen years earlier. The rest of the books he had been so carefully purchasing would have to stay, as would most of his art and scientific supplies. *But speed and mobility may be far more critical this trip than it was then*, he thought sadly.

Carefully packing up some of the precious notebooks he had been keeping for years, he turned to Luca. He couldn't help grimacing at his own proposal: "We can go first to Mantua. Beatrice's older sister Isabella has been after me for some time to come and paint her portrait. Surely she would welcome old friends of her sister at this difficult time. And in spite of her idiosyncrasies, it could be a temporary haven for us."

Travel Years – Overview

When Duke Ludovico lost Milan to the French in 1499, Leonardo left the city searching for new employment. He would spend many of the next six years wandering across Italy, during which time he did very little artistic work, but a significant amount of scientific work. He traveled first to Mantua, and then on to Venice, and eventually he returned to Florence for a brief stay.

In 1502, he took one of his most unusual assignments, working for Cesare Borgia, military dictator for almost a year, traveling throughout the region of Romagna during much of that time. During that same year, he submitted plans to the Ottoman Sultan for a bridge the Sultan wanted to build over the mouth of the Black Sea.

When Leonardo tired of that work, he took a commission in Florence, and returned there, as a "local hero." During the next few years he traveled between Florence and Milan several times, often in an attempt to settle family issues caused by the lack of a will,[57] or a contested will.[58]

Leonardo's most significant artwork during this time was his famous *Mona Lisa* painting.

---

[57] *At his father's death.*
[58] *After his uncle's death.*

Travel Years - Leonardo, the Military Advisor

"If the fortress can be attacked only from a single side, make that side in the form of a massive acute angle of 25 – 30 feet, with its lateral defenses…"

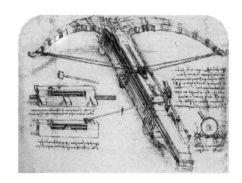

From 1499 – 1502, Cesare Borgia, son of Pope Alexander VI and military dictator, was ruthless in his attempt to gain power over Romagna, a central portion of Italy.[59] He was encouraged in his efforts by the Pope. Leonardo worked for Borgia as "senior military architect and general engineer" during much of that time, and met Niccolo Machiavelli, who was also working for Borgia. (Many years later Machiavelli would write his most famous book, *The Prince*, significantly based on the unscrupulous means by which Borgia conquered and ruled.)

As advisor to Borgia, Leonardo traveled throughout central Italy – Imola, Cesena, Rimini, Urbino, and Pesaro. He gave recommendations for military improvements, as well as accurately mapping the region. Later he was in Piombino to improve the fortifications of the town Borgia had just taken from Jacopo Appiani.

Later, back in Florence, Leonardo worked with Machiavelli for over a year trying to divert the Arno River with canals, for military and transportation purposes. It would have involved tunneling through the Serravalle Mountain Pass.[60]

---

[59] *Italy was not a unified country at the time – it was mostly comprised of independent city-states who were constantly fighting each other for power, as well as fighting France, Spain, Germany, and the Ottoman Empire.*
[60] *The tunneling and canals were not done until modern times, and Leonardo's exact route was used.*

After the downfall of Borgia, Leonardo went back to Piombino briefly. Here Machiavelli was attempting a diplomatic mission, when Leonardo came to advise the new/old leader, Appiani, on the city's fortifications. Leonardo's recommendations included a tunnel or moat, trenches, and the leveling of some hills outside the fortifications. He also planned for some improvements to the towers, including the placement of cannon there (He was the first military architect to suggest that).

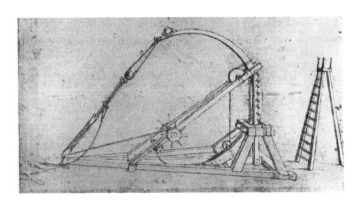

For a man who despised war, Leonardo spent much time advising those who practiced it![61]

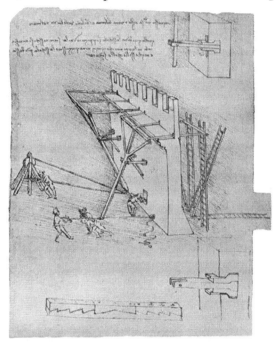

[61] *Possibly out of a false sense of loyalty, but more likely for the money – since he frequently needed to worry about who his next patron would be.*

Leonardo da Vinci, Military Advisor

(Doing Da Vinci)

"If by reason of the height of the banks, or the strength of the place and its position, it is impossible, when besieging a place, to avail oneself of the plan of bombardment, I have methods for destroying every rock or other fortress, even if it were founded on a rock, etc."

Student Activity

After sketching a variety of military ideas, we worked on our own designs/models of catapults and trebuchets using cardboard, cardboard rolls, plastic spoons, rubber bands, and tape.

We also enjoyed portions of Nova's video: *Medieval Siege* from the Secrets of Lost Empires series. It shows two groups designing and testing different trebuchets based on medieval designs.

Leonardo made a practice of always carrying a small notebook with him and then copying his notes, sketches, etc. onto larger sheets each evening. His notebooks were generally unorganized, usually consisting of loose pages, that he only occasionally bound himself. They included notes on countless things, including ideas for weapons.

Even though Leonardo hated war, and considered himself a pacifist, many of his ideas were for tools useful in military operations:
- Diving Bell
- Diving Suit
- Flying Ship
- Hang Glider
- Helicopter
- Horseless Wagon
- Machine Gun
- Naval Cannon
- Parachute
- Pontoon Bridges
- Revolving Bridge
- Submarine
- Tank
- Temporary Bridges

In fact, when Leonardo was looking for a job with Duke Ludovico, he emphasized his ideas for offensive and defensive war machines more than his artistic abilities.

Leonardo's Work as a Military Advisor

U	H	U	F	L	Y	I	N	G	S	H	I	P	F	S	E	N
E	R	A	R	O	N	U	G	E	N	I	H	C	A	M	D	O
X	N	O	N	A	N	G	J	P	R	X	H	N	O	I	N	G
T	L	Z	S	G	X	A	A	Y	Z	L	V	K	V	E	I	A
K	B	G	D	J	G	R	V	G	T	U	I	I	N	R	D	W
E	X	Y	E	Z	A	L	R	A	D	K	N	X	E	A	D	S
H	N	K	T	C	J	P	I	P	L	G	B	T	G	U	T	S
A	J	I	H	S	G	G	U	D	B	C	P	F	Z	O	N	E
K	J	U	R	Y	F	C	E	A	E	O	A	Z	Z	N	D	L
O	T	Y	R	A	O	X	L	F	C	R	C	N	C	C	N	E
E	U	B	I	Y	M	L	N	I	P	B	Y	A	N	N	X	S
O	A	F	Z	D	Z	B	L	O	P	S	J	N	X	O	M	R
A	R	E	R	A	G	E	U	W	K	N	C	O	Z	Z	N	O
D	L	P	P	B	H	P	W	S	C	C	E	Y	N	J	F	H
T	O	Z	F	O	B	P	O	N	T	O	O	N	B	O	A	T
X	H	S	O	T	I	U	S	G	N	I	V	I	D	W	Q	Q

1. Tank
2. Hang Glider
3. Horseless Wagon
4. Pontoon Boat
5. Helicopter
6. Parachute

7. Machine Gun
8. Diving Suit
9. Submarine
10. Flying Ship
11. Naval Cannon

Where Did Leonardo Work as a Military Advisor?

C	M	M	X	Z	S	Q	A	R	N	R	W	N	H	K	S	F
S	E	R	R	A	V	A	L	L	E	M	T	N	P	A	S	S
A	H	G	K	J	W	D	E	Y	O	T	T	A	M	Q	Z	O
C	B	E	U	R	O	I	P	Y	P	M	D	N	U	Y	W	Q
W	Z	C	R	S	J	L	D	N	L	G	I	G	L	D	Q	Z
D	P	B	B	C	G	H	W	B	Y	N	O	A	D	R	P	M
I	E	C	I	H	E	Q	L	N	X	H	T	M	I	J	I	V
G	S	F	N	L	S	S	P	Q	R	I	J	O	T	L	O	N
F	A	R	O	H	O	H	E	E	I	S	P	R	M	C	M	M
L	R	A	G	V	L	B	V	N	M	E	L	A	X	I	B	D
O	O	T	N	L	C	I	J	L	A	O	C	J	T	N	I	Y
R	R	X	P	D	R	A	F	W	X	A	K	U	Y	A	N	R
E	M	W	C	O	L	R	A	I	N	I	M	I	R	L	O	T
N	J	V	N	G	J	W	G	C	O	J	U	T	C	I	O	Y
C	E	R	I	N	M	R	V	O	F	J	G	Q	X	M	M	P
E	A	B	S	E	K	C	N	I	O	E	V	Z	D	F	T	L

1. Piombino
2. Pesaro
3. Milan
4. Cesena
5. Romagna

6. Arno River
7. Florence
8. Imola
9. Rimini
10. Urbino

Travel Years - Leonardo's Bridge

"I have plans for bridges..."

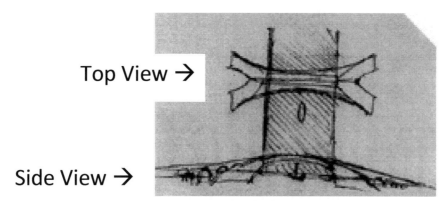

Top View →

Side View →

Leonardo was offered another unique assignment while working for Cesare Borgia. This time it was Sultan Bajazet II, ruler of the Ottoman Empire, who considered hiring him.

The Sultan had sent ambassadors to the region of Italy to find engineers to design a bridge over the Bosphorus, or Golden Horn, at the mouth of the Black Sea. Leonardo drew up plans for the Sultan's bridge, shown on the next page. The Sultan and his advisors thought Leonardo's bridge, a giant arch shape, [62] was too radical, and that it would not be strong enough in the middle. [63]

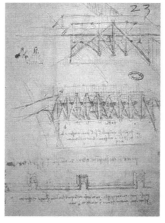

Throughout his long and varied career, da Vinci made other plans for bridges as well.

Leonardo was so convinced of his design that he offered to build the bridge himself. Instead, the Sultan requested that Leonardo's rival, Michelangelo, submit an alternate set of plans, but Michelangelo was busy in Rome, and declined the offer. The Sultan never got his bridge built – and bridges were not built across the Golden Horn for over three hundred years – until 1836 and 1845.

---

[62] *You have to look closely at the bottom portion of the drawing to see the arch shape.*
[63] *Had it been built, at almost 1100 feet in length, it would have been the longest bridge of its day.*

LEONARDO DA VINCI'S BRIDGE(S)

(Doing Da Vinci)

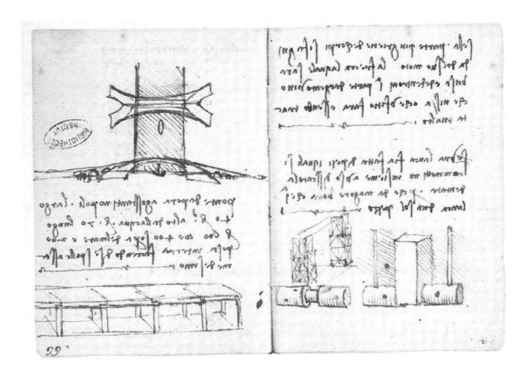

"I have a sort of extremely light and strong bridges, adapted to be most easily carried..."

Student Activities

First, we studied the different architectural styles of bridges through the ages, comparing and contrasting them.

Then we sketched bridges on our own, and then worked on our bridge models, using cardboard, paper, straws, toothpicks, and popsicle sticks.

Leonardo's Bridge

I	I	M	R	U	Y	E	Q	M	U	Z	A	L	A	J	X	Q
S	U	L	T	A	N	B	A	J	A	Z	E	T	I	I	V	T
N	S	D	W	J	S	F	Z	C	Y	P	X	E	G	E	X	F
K	F	R	N	E	M	I	C	H	E	L	A	N	G	E	L	O
M	O	Q	H	A	W	Y	N	O	I	S	N	E	P	S	U	S
N	H	C	B	S	S	R	U	I	H	Z	T	U	Z	X	G	T
U	R	K	I	O	A	M	R	U	L	D	E	V	A	U	H	I
A	Q	J	R	A	R	G	O	L	D	E	N	H	O	R	N	M
G	D	E	G	P	F	G	Y	J	Q	T	C	J	G	N	A	B
D	A	O	A	Q	A	U	I	R	B	W	C	K	L	S	F	E
L	V	R	I	T	D	W	G	A	U	E	Z	V	D	D	Y	R
A	I	N	C	U	J	X	B	Z	Y	A	V	N	L	F	M	T
M	N	W	E	R	I	P	M	E	N	A	M	O	T	T	O	R
M	C	P	U	C	I	L	C	Y	E	G	D	I	R	B	V	U
E	I	A	J	N	O	S	N	E	E	U	Q	R	B	H	R	S
T	I	M	B	E	R	C	A	N	T	I	L	E	V	E	R	S

1. Golden Horn	8. Michelangelo
2. Ottoman Empire	9. Borgia
3. Suspension	10. Norway
4. Da Vinci	11. Sultan Bajazet II
5. Bridge	12. Queen Sonja
6. Timber Truss	13. Timber Cantilever
7. Arches	14. Vebjorn Sand

In addition to his artwork, which he was so famous for, Leonardo spent much of his time on various types of design work. His designs included bridges at different times in his career, including when he wrote his letter/resume to the Duke of Milan. The first portion of the letter, where he refers to bridges is included below:

To My Lord the Duke of Milan,
Florence,1482

Most Illustrious Lord,

Having until now sufficiently considered the specimens of all those who proclaim themselves skilled contrivers of instruments of war, and that the invention and operation of the said instruments are nothing different to those in common use: I shall endeavor, without prejudice to anyone else, to explain myself to your Excellency showing your Lordship my secrets, and then offering them to your best pleasure and approbation to work with effect at opportune moments as well as all those things which in part, shall be briefly noted below:

> *I have a sort of extremely light and strong* **bridges,** *adapted to be most easily carried, and with them you may pursue, and at any time flee from the enemy; and others, secure and indestructible by fire and battle, easy and convenient to lift and place. Also methods to burn and destroy those of the enemy.*

I know how, when a place is besieged, to take the water out of the trenches, and make endless variety of **bridges,** *and covered ways and ladders, and other machines pertaining to such expeditions.*

His notebooks included designs for a Swing Bridge, a Retractable Bridge, and a Self-Supporting Bridge. Leonardo's bridge for the Sultan was forgotten about for many centuries until a Norwegian artist saw the plans at a Leonardo da Vinci exhibit in 1996, and fell in love with Leonardo's idea.

The Norwegian artist, Vebjorn Sand, convinced the Norwegian Highway Department to build a scaled down version of the bridge. In 2002, Norwegian Queen Sonja, unveiled the beautiful arch bridge, designed 500 years earlier by Leonardo da Vinci. Sand now hopes to build one of the bridges on every continent.

Other arch bridges throughout the ages, and throughout the world, have included:

Puente Alcantara, a Roman stone-arch bridge in Spain, from the 1ˢᵗ Century.

*This **Chinese Camel-Back Arched Bridge** from the 12ᵗʰ century.*

Other popular bridge styles have included:

*This **timber cantilever bridge** in India was constructed during the 19ᵗʰ century.*

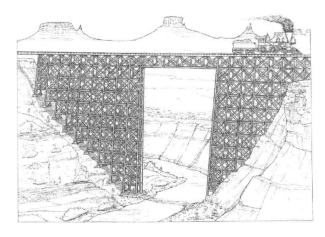

*This **timber-truss railroad bridge** was a popular bridge type in the westward expansion of the United States during the same time period, the late 19ᵗʰ century.*

Modern bridges are often suspension bridges. Two famous examples of those include:

***The Brooklyn Bridge** in New York City, was the longest suspension bridge in the world when it was completed in 1883.*

***The Golden Gate Bridge** in San Francisco was the longest suspension bridge in the world when it was completed in 1937.*

Travel Years - *Battle of Anghiari* Painting

Leonardo on how to represent a battle: "First you must represent the smoke of artillery mingling in the air with the dust and tossed up by the movement of horses and the combatants. And this mixture you must express thus..."

In 1503, city officials in Florence wanted frescos painted on the walls of their new City Hall, and invited the now famous Leonardo and Michelangelo to paint them. It became a contest of sorts between the two painters, who did not get along particularly well.[64] Leonardo chose to paint the *Battle of Anghiari* on his wall, and Michelangelo went to work on the *Battle of Cascina*.[65] (These wall frescoes were to be more than twice as large as *The Last Supper* fresco, which Leonardo had already completed.)[66]

Both Michelangelo and Leonardo prepared their initial "cartoons"[67] fairly quickly – to show how they intended to paint their walls. Leonardo especially wanted to insure that he had the angry faces of battle correct, the horses in the right positions, etc. He would not even begin painting the wall for almost two years.

Unfortunately, Leonardo chose another experimental technique, since he was still not happy with the available fresco techniques. This time the problem was that the paint would not dry. To correct the situation, Leonardo had assistants raise pots of hot oil on ropes up and down next to the wall. Unfortunately, the paint did not dry in the process – it ran instead, completely obliterating the painting Leonardo had done. Rather than go back and fix his mess, Leonardo just walked away from the job. Michelangelo never finished his wall either, being called off to Rome before he completed it. All that remains of the paintings are the sketches in Leonardo's notebook and copies of the walls painted by contemporary artists.

The city officials of Florence would later complain that Leonardo had taken money for payment for a project he didn't finish. Eventually Leonardo would offer to pay the money back, and the officials would graciously decline.

---

[64] *Among other things, Michelangelo, the "young upstart," had mocked Leonardo for his failed equestrian monument.*

[65] *Both were important victories against Pisa in Florence's past.*

[66] *23 x 56 feet*

[67] *Their large sketches showing the way the compositions would be painted.*

Leonardo's Flight

X	F	E	R	J	Z	R	S	N	B	F	R	H	O	U	R	E
O	L	F	T	T	X	G	D	B	H	E	M	H	K	E	M	X
R	Y	E	V	U	Y	B	R	K	T	C	E	T	E	A	Z	R
N	I	M	C	F	H	J	Y	P	D	A	V	I	N	C	I	M
I	N	S	L	N	I	C	O	Z	W	M	X	G	G	D	X	M
T	G	V	S	M	A	C	A	G	M	X	O	H	S	P	O	K
H	M	N	C	P	I	T	W	R	Q	M	W	O	X	Z	F	B
O	A	K	M	L	C	X	S	Z	A	I	S	T	H	K	H	D
P	C	P	E	X	N	J	G	I	N	P	K	D	T	Q	R	E
T	H	H	U	K	R	B	I	G	S	L	S	W	R	A	K	Z
E	I	Z	E	T	I	K	S	L	U	E	R	O	W	I	D	U
R	N	U	I	U	E	X	I	W	T	U	R	Y	F	C	B	B
A	E	R	I	A	L	S	C	R	E	W	K	D	X	I	A	Z
W	L	Z	B	N	Y	J	O	I	X	S	Y	U	N	T	Y	M
H	R	E	D	I	L	G	Z	G	K	F	G	F	S	I	C	O
D	C	B	W	U	Y	O	M	V	G	L	Y	O	W	G	W	N

1. Aerial
2. Screw
3. Helicopter
4. Ornithopter
5. Birds
6. Flying Machine
7. Parachute Wings
8. Da Vinci
9. Skyward
10. Glider
11. Wind Resistance
12. Bats
13. Kite

Travel Years - Leonardo and Flight

"Feathers shall raise men even as they do birds..."

Leonardo da Vinci was fascinated by flight and the idea of humans flying. He spent much time observing birds in flight, and dreaming of ways to fly. He analyzed how they flew, and the effects of wind and air resistance on their wings. Many of his notebook pages dealing with flight are dated 1505. In 1508 one of his assistants was injured, trying out one of Leonardo's flying contraptions.

In the East, kites had been in existence long before Leonardo's day, and sometimes he is mistakenly credited for "inventing" them in the West. There is no proof of this, but rather it results from confusion caused by a story from his early childhood: "...among the reflections of my infancy, it seemed to me that, as I was in my cradle, a kite came to me...and struck me several times with its tail..." This kite, in his story, was a bird, in the hawk family!

Leonardo drew designs for a helicopter and a parachute. And even though he would not live to see men fly, his ideas and designs are often listed first in studies of "the history of flight." Four hundred years after Leonardo da Vinci drew flying contraptions in the pages of his notebooks, the Wright brothers realized his dream of flying.

LEONARDO DA VINCI AND FLIGHT
(Doing Da Vinci)

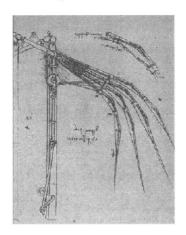

"When once you have tasted flight, you will forever walk the earth with your eyes turned skyward, for there you have been, and there you will always long to return."

"Feathers shall raise men even as they do birds..."

Student Activity

After sketching flight ideas, the students took their turn at designing parachutes and paper airplanes. For their parachutes, students picked from plastic bags, paper towels, straws, yarn, paperclips, craft sticks, and coffee filters.

Leonardo da Vinci was fascinated by flight, and the idea of humans flying. He spent much time observing birds and bats in flight, analyzing how they flew, and the effects of wind and air resistance on their wings. Leonardo dreamt of developing ways for man to fly.

Leonardo's "Ornithopter
A Glider Designed so a Human Could Fly with His Own Power

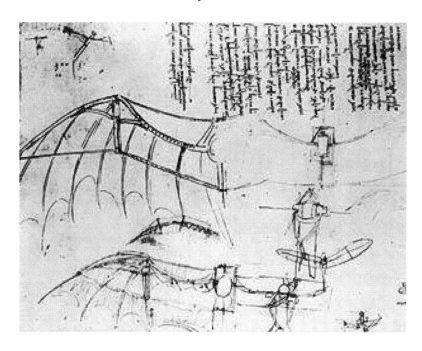

Leonardo's "Flying Machines"
(It would be another 400 years before successful gliders were built.)

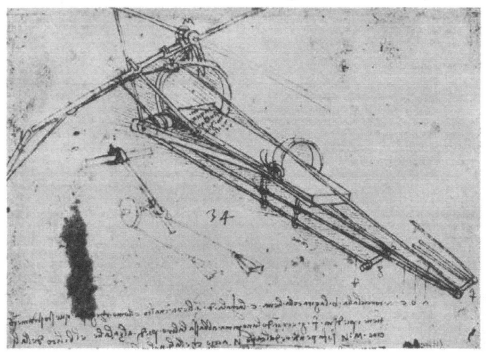

The Aerial Screw
Considered the forerunner to the Helicopter:

Leonardo said of it: *"I believe that if this screw device is well manufactured, that is, if it is made of linen cloth, the pores of which have been closed with starch, and if the device is promptly reversed, the screw will engage its gear when in the air and it will rise up on high"*

400 years later, shortly after the Wright Brothers had successfully flown their first airplane, a Frenchman flew the first helicopter.

Leonardo's Parachute
The right dimensions, but not the "right shape":

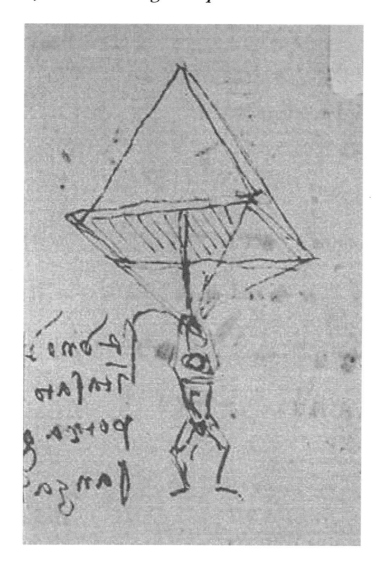

"If a man is provided with a length of gummed linen cloth - linen fabric treated in such a way as to have all interstices filled - with a length of twelve yards on each side and twelve yards high, he can jump from any great height whatsoever, without any injury to his body."
Leonardo da Vinci

Three hundred years later a Frenchman would successfully use a parachute – jumping from a hot air balloon.

And even though he would not live to see men fly, his ideas and designs are often listed first in studies of "the history of flight." Four hundred years after Leonardo da Vinci drew flying contraptions in the pages of his notebooks, the Wright brothers realized his dream of flying.

Mona Lisa, *otherwise known as* "La Gioconda" *or* "La Joconde."

Travel Years - *Mona Lisa*

"Let your shadings melt away like smoke, like the sounds of soft music."

68

After attending eight classes and two workshops about Leonardo da Vinci, my ten-year-old has decided to write her own book on Leonardo. Her book currently begins: "Leonardo was a famous artist. Most of the reason he was so famous is because of the Mona Lisa, his most beloved of all..."

It is an intriguing picture – the smile, the veil, the hands that hold nothing, the unusual landscape in the background, the position of the sitter...In fact, the *Mona Lisa* is perhaps the single most famous painting in the world, but it is a surprisingly small painting, measuring only 21" X 30."[69] Its fame and mystery far exceed its size.

On a recent trip to Italy we were told that this is the building where da Vinci painted the Mona Lisa.

The first debate about this intriguing work is over the identity of the woman in the painting.[70] Most (but not all) historians[71] agree that she was Lisa, the wife of Franceso del Giocondo,[72] from whence comes our English name for the picture.[73] Her smile has also intrigued people

---

[68] *These hands are considered by some to be from Leonardo's sketches for the Mona Lisa. For some reason, there are no other sketches in Leonardo's notebooks that go with the Mona Lisa. And yet, there seems to be no question as to its authenticity as "a da Vinci." One possibility is that the sketches he made for it are in the 7,000 or so pages missing from his notebooks!*

[69] *Or 53 cm X 77 cm*

[70] *Some art critics have gone so far as to say that the painting is really a self-portrait of Leonardo. I've even seen computerized images trying to prove that point. I don't believe a word of it!*

[71] *Starting with Leonardo's first biographer, Giorgio Vasari, in 1547, who dedicated ten pages of his Great Lives of Artists book to Leonardo da Vinci (Michelangelo received seventy-five).*

[72] *Lisa would have been an "upper middle class" Florentine lady, wife and mother.*

[73] *The Italians call her La Gioconda and the French call her La Joconde.*

for a long time; Leonardo may have employed musicians to keep her happy during her sitting time.

The next mystery is why Leonardo never gave up the painting during his lifetime. He had been commissioned to paint it while still living in Italy, and he worked on it for at least four years there,[74] but it was one of the three paintings he took with him when he moved to France. [75] He apparently never considered it completed, or at least that's what he kept telling the man who had contracted with him for the picture! It is possible that he continued to work on it off and on during all those years. That certainly would have fit with his personality and work style.

King Francis I was very impressed with the painting, and offered to buy it from Leonardo. Leonardo was reluctant to part with it, but also wanted to please his new patron.[76] They struck an interesting deal: The king paid for the painting, but Leonardo kept it in his new home in France, and when Leonardo died, the king took possession of it. Which is why the most famous painting in the world was painted by an Italian, but hangs in a French museum.[77]

Of course, it didn't begin its "career" as the most famous painting in the world, it had to work its way up to that position. Even in Leonardo's lifetime it was a popular painting, Raphael had seen it while Leonardo was still working on it, and was impressed by it. Other painters were soon copying it. Soon after Leonardo's death, the biographer Vasari was already referring to it as a masterpiece.

But, during its first centuries in France, it became "just another painting by a master." It was not even considered by most to be Leonardo's best painting. Sometime after Leonardo's death it eventually moved with King Francis I from Amboise to his newly renovated Fontainebleau. The *Mona Lisa* eventually made it to the palace at Versailles where it spent almost two centuries. The Louvre was opened it 1793, and in 1797, the *Mona Lisa* was moved with the other masterpieces from the Versailles to the Louvre. As the Louvre became more accessible to everyday folks, the *Mona Lisa's* popularity slowly began to rise.

In the mid-1800's its standing among masterpieces was slowly increasing. And in the late 1800's, with the help of an ever increasing international press, *Mona Lisa's* smile began receiving attention.

And then one day, in the days of less-stringent security in the Louvre, something happened to greatly increase the *Mona Lisa's* popularity. On a Sunday in 1911 an Italian man, Vincenzo Peruggia, was working in the museum. But on this day, instead of leaving after the work day,

---

[74] *Leonardo spent as much time on this one small painting as Michelangelo had spent on an entire ceiling fresco.*

[75] *The other two pictures were St John the Baptist and the Virgin and Child with Saint Anne.*

[76] *His new employer.*

[77] *The Louvre was opened in 1793, and in 1797 the Mona Lisa was sent there with the other paintings from the Versailles. (From 1800 to 1804, it hung in Napoleon's private quarters, instead of the Louvre.)*

he hid in a closet. The next day the museum was closed. He came out of the closet, took the *Mona Lisa* off the wall and out of its frame, and left the museum with the painting hidden under his clothes.[78]

The theft was not even discovered until the following day, after the museum had opened again. A local artist had come to the museum, as was his custom, to paint a copy of the *Mona Lisa*.[79] As he was setting up his equipment, he realized that the *Mona Lisa* was not hanging in her spot on the wall. He enquired of a guard as to where the painting had gone. The guard assumed the painting had been removed to the museum photo studio to be photographed. Time passed and the painting did not return. The local painter finally bribed the guard to go check on it. Lo and behold, it was not there. The museum was immediately sealed off as a search for the missing painting began. Alas, it was gone. People leaving Paris and France were searched for the painting as well, but it was not discovered.[80]

The robbery made headline news across the world. People mourned for the *Mona Lisa*, songs were written to her, flowers were brought to her empty spot at the museum. And for two years, the clues to her disappearance were almost non-existent: museum security blamed the Paris police for not finding more clues, and of course the police blamed the museum for having bad security. Rumors flew. One was that a rich millionaire from the U.S. had paid to have the painting stolen, and another that the Germans had stolen it to make the French look bad. (World War I was lurking in the not-too distant future.)

Those rumors were all eventually shown to be incorrect. Two years after its disappearance, after most had given up on ever seeing the painting again, an Italian art dealer placed a routine ad that he was looking for good art to buy. He received a mysterious response to his ad – from a "Leonardo" who claimed to have the *Mona Lisa* for sale. Needless to say the art dealer was a bit suspicious – many folks had claimed to have the painting during the previous two years. The dealer showed up at the apartment of the man who claimed to have the *Mona Lisa*. He brought with him a friend from the local art museum. "Leonardo" unpacked a large crate, removed a false bottom, and then removed the painting. Lo and behold, it was the *Mona Lisa* (as proven by the Louvre seal on the back of the painting).

Playing it cool, the two art experts informed "Leonardo" that they would have to take the painting with them to compare it to some of Leonardo's other work, to check its authenticity. The thief allowed them to leave the apartment with the painting, at which time they promptly called the police and he was arrested. As a loyal Italian, he claimed he only wanted the painting back in Italy "where it belonged"! (After his trial, he spent less than a year in jail, of the three years the prosecuting lawyer had asked for – and to this day it is unknown whether he actually worked alone, as he claimed he had done.)

---

[78] He could not have rolled the picture, like the thief in *Ever After*. It was painted on poplar wood.

[79] He routinely did this, and sold the copies to visitors.

[80] The painting remained in hiding for two years (possibly in France the entire time).

After her rediscovery, the *Mona Lisa* was taken on tour to several major cities in Italy and then returned to her home in France. She stayed there without incident for the next fifty years or so, except during World War II when she was removed from the Louvre along with other important artwork and moved numerous times to avoid destruction or theft.

The next time *Mona Lisa* came out of the Louvre was in a political move. John F. Kennedy was the U.S. president, and the French were much enamored with the Kennedy family. France decided to grant the United States' request to "borrow" the *Mona Lisa* for a short time. A special packing crate was made for her and she was shipped to the United States under heavy security. She was exhibited in Washington D.C. for several weeks, and then was taken to New York City for display. Over 1 ½ million Americans viewed the painting at the two locations before she was returned to her spot in France.

In 1974, *Mona Lisa* traveled by plane to Tokyo and then Moscow, and was seen by two million viewers. It was for this journey that a special bullet proof case was made for the *Mona Lisa*, and she remains in it, the only painting in the Louvre that is so protected. Then the painting was returned to her home in France, where she remains to this day.

Before her theft, *Mona Lisa* was already considered a world-class painting. But since her theft and recovery, the painting's fame across the world has increased significantly. The *Mona Lisa* became the subject of an increasing number of poems, stories, and songs, while "the smile" became a bigger and bigger part of her fame.

Today, most who think of Leonardo da Vinci, think first of his *Mona Lisa*, and most who think of her, think immediately of her smile.

Travel Years - Leonardo and Nature Studies

"If you wish to represent a tempest, consider its effects as seen and arrange well, when the wind, blowing over the face of the sea and earth, removes and carries with it such things as are not fixed to the general mass."

From Leonardo's youth, he was fascinated by severe weather – tornados, earthquakes, and the like. He did countless drawings showing the effects of severe storms. One of his first drawings was a landscape drawing, which was very unusual for his time period. As he drew he observed: *"Mountains are made by the currents of rivers. Mountains are destroyed by the currents of rivers."*

As Leonardo studied all that was around him, he asked: *"Why do we find the bones of great fishes and oysters and corals and various other shells and sea-snails on the high summits of mountains by the sea, just as we find them in low seas?"* (Leonardo didn't believe in Creation, or even "the great flood," but he constantly struggled to get his observations to match his beliefs.)

As much imagination as Leonardo must have had to do everything he did, his artwork came from real life – oftentimes nature. Leonardo also drew many plants in his notebooks, studying the specimens intently as he drew them.

Botany quickly became another side interest, and Leonardo noted:
"A leaf always turns its upper side towards the sky so that it may better receive, on all its surface, the dew which drops gently from the atmosphere."

 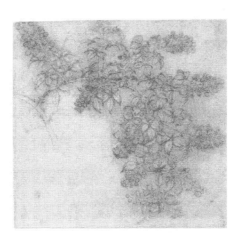 

Even when he drew imaginary animals, Leonardo used real animals as his models.

Another story from Leonardo's youth goes like this: While he was still living in Vinci, his father was given the commission for painting a shield. Leonardo painted an imaginary animal on the shield that was very scary.[81] He positioned it in such a way that his father saw the animal without realizing he was looking at a painting – and he was scared! Leonardo had succeeded.[82]

He especially liked horses and birds. He would often buy caged birds, just so that he could set them free. His notebooks show lots of sketches of horses and birds, and occasionally other animals.

In fact, Leonardo liked animals so much that he became a vegetarian, which was very unusual in those days.

---

[81] *Though the animal was imaginary, Leonardo had used the features of several different real animals to make it.*
[82] *His father would go on to sell the shield for much money, and deliver a different shield to the man who had originally commissioned him.*

139

Leonardo da Vinci and Nature Studies

(Doing Da Vinci)

"Human subtlety will never devise an invention more beautiful, more simple or more direct than does nature because in her inventions nothing is lacking, and nothing is superfluous."

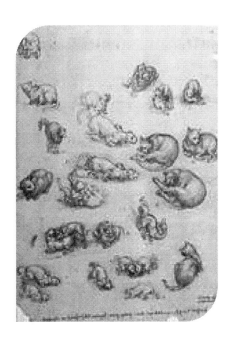

Student Activities

We started by discussing what Nature is. Leonardo's interest in Nature included Weather, Plants, Animals, and Landscapes.

We read and discussed fables by Leonardo, Aesop, and Rudyard Kipling.

We made sketches of animals and clay models of animals. Some also made habitats for their animals. Students were then encouraged to write an animal poem and/or and animal fables.

In the spirit of Leonardo's observation of plants, we also did leaf rubbings, and sketches of plants.

"The smallest feline is a masterpiece."

Travel Years - Leonardo's Fables and Tales

"Consult nature in everything and write it down."

Like Aesop before him, and Rudyard Kipling after him, Leonardo liked to write short stories, typically with animals as the subjects, and a moral message as a conclusion. His fables and tales were often pointed, and often humorous, though not always student-friendly! One of his many fables: "A rat was confined in his little home by a weasel, who with unwearied patience awaited his surrender. Suddenly a cat came and seized the weasel and immediately ate it. The rat came out of his hole quickly to give thanks for his new freedom and revel in his newly regained liberty. But he was instantly stripped of both, together with his life, by the ferocious claws and teeth of the cat who waited outside his hole."[83]

After reading Leonardo's fables, one of my students, David Cox, wrote his own: "There was once a lazy fly who loved macaroni, but he hated making it. So he decided to try to trick someone else into making macaroni for him. He decided to put up a sign on the town bulletin. The sign read, 'Help Wanted'. Later that day, the fly gets a call, 'I'll help.' So at 7:00 the spider came over to help make the mac and cheese and eats the fly and the macaroni and cheese. The moral of this story is: Make your own mac and cheese."

Leonardo also wrote many humorous tales. One of them went something like this: "A man was instructed to rise from bed, since the sun was already risen. He responded: 'If I had as far to go, and as much to do as he has, I should be risen by now; but having but a little way to go, I shall not rise yet.'"[84]

---

[83] *This fable is one of the nineteen fables in The Notebooks of Leonardo da Vinci, Volume 1.*
[84] *The tale is also in The Notebooks of Leonardo da Vinci, Volume 1.*

Travel Years - Leonardo and Anatomy

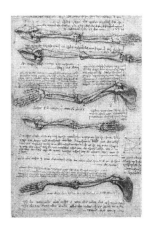

"The painter who is familiar with the nature of the sinews, muscles, and tendons, will know very well, in giving movement to a limb, how many and which sinews cause it."

Leonardo da Vinci merged art and science throughout his life. His understanding of optics led him to improvements in shadows and perspective in painting, and his knowledge of geology and geography improved the quality of the landscapes he drew and painted. And his knowledge of anatomy improved the realism in the human figures he drew and painted.

Anatomy is the study of the structure of living things. Leonardo da Vinci was very interested in anatomy because it allowed him to be a better painter. As he studied the human body, plants, and animals, he was able to draw and paint them more accurately.

Leonardo's anatomical studies are among his greatest contributions to science. Here his artistic ability is combined with his observation skills and imagination. In fact, in his time he was considered by some to be the greatest anatomist in the world. He is credited with being the first to make anatomical drawings in the manner still used today – using four sketches to show each part. He was the first to make cross-sectional drawings of the body showing veins, arteries, and nerves in this manner. Thus he was the first to make anatomy studies truly a visual science, relying primarily on an abundance of pictures rather than words. One of Leonardo's most incredible drawings is that of the "Embryo in the Womb." It takes my breath away to see something so "pro-life" that was drawn 500 years ago!

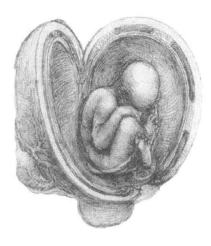

Leonardo actually knew more about the workings of the human body than most doctors in his day. As a painter, he was particularly interested in the way the eyes worked. To see was to perceive, was to be able to draw... Leonardo also studied the skeletal system. And in the last years of his life he studied the heart. He began his study of the heart with studies of cows' hearts. He compared the flow of blood to the flow of water.

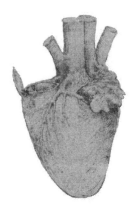

Over the years, Leonardo dissected animals occasionally, including bears, cows, frogs, horses, monkeys, and pigs, though he preferred to do human dissections.

Leonardo drew his "Vitruvian Man"[85] to show the "ideal proportions" of the human body. He based those proportions on his studies of the human body through the years, and the measurements he had taken. It was not an idea that originated with Leonardo – but once again he was the one who took it to a higher level. His notebooks contain countless entries describing the various proportions he had observed and measured.

In 1507, after witnessing the death of an old man at a hospital in Florence, Leonardo's interest was sparked again. The old man died very peaceably, and Leonardo was allowed to do a study of his body in an attempt to determine why the man had died.

Leonardo did a few more human dissections during the first few years of his anatomy studies, moving up to more than ten in 1509 alone.

For a short period of time, probably from 1510 – 1511, Leonardo did dissections with Della Torra, an anatomy professor, and the leading anatomist of their age, at the University in Pavia, near Milan. By time he died, da Vinci had done more than thirty human dissections and had completed thousands of anatomical drawings.

Leonardo had kept his anatomical studies mostly a secret during his life time. In 1510 he made plans to publish his anatomy studies of the entire human body, plans that were never carried out.

---

[85] *Shown in Appendix A.*

LEONARDO DA VINCI AND THE HUMAN BODY

(Doing Da Vinci)

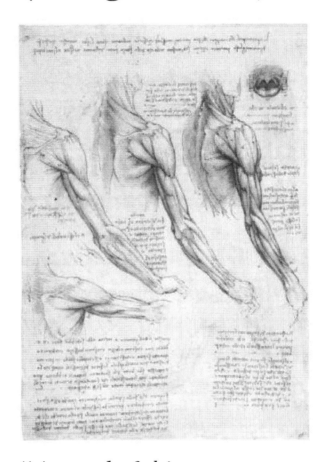

*"A wonderful instrument,
the invention of the supreme master."*

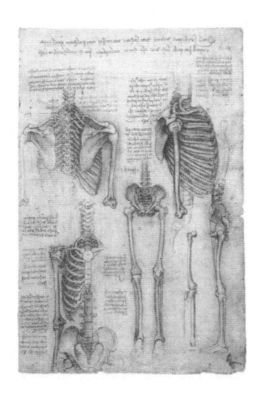

Student Activities

We discussed da Vinci's dissection work, and his interest in anatomy as it helped him with his art.

Then we focused on his Vitruvian Man and the human proportions he observed. Splitting the class up into groups of two or three, we had the students measure each other to fill out the Human Proportions chart (Appendix A). Then we compared everyone's results, and discovered when da Vinci's predictions were accurate.

Final Years – Overview

Leonardo da Vinci was in Rome from 1514 to 1516. Leonardo had hoped to join Michelangelo and Raphael doing great artwork for the Pope, the head of the Roman Catholic Church, but his reputation of not completing projects had preceded him, and the Pope wasn't interested in hiring him. Leonardo did more of his scientific work in those years in Rome.

He also traveled to Pavia, Bologna, and Milan during that time.

In 1515, Leonardo was accused of sorcery, because of his work dissecting dead bodies. At that point, the Pope, as the "law of the land," banned Leonardo from performing any further human dissections.

During that time there were several other artists in Rome doing work for the Pope, and Donato Bramante was building St. Peters Cathedral. But, apparently Leonardo had little contact with the other artists at this time, and may have been quite lonely at this period of his life. This may have contributed to his acceptance when the King of France offered him a new job, in France.

Leonardo built a mechanical lion in 1515 for the celebrations in conjunction with the coronation of Francis I, King of France. The lion was capable of movement; and when it opened its mouth, it revealed lilies. Leonardo's lion was written about in other contemporary accounts, not just his own.

In 1515, the new French King, Francis I, traveled into northern Italy to prove his strength against those in that area. Francis I was the French king who had formed a large royal library and appointed a royal librarian. He had a deep interest in the arts and sciences. While in Italy, he met Leonardo da Vinci and invited him to France.

Final Years - Leonardo in Rome

Of his mint at Rome, Leonardo said, *"It can also be made without a spring. But the screw above must always be joined to the part of the movable sheath…all the coins should be a perfect circle."*

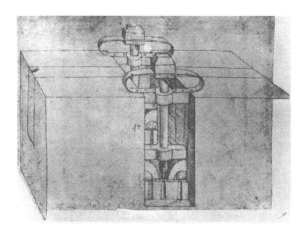

Leonardo da Vinci moved to Rome under the patronage of Giuliano de Medici, brother of Pope Leo X.

Leonardo opened an art studio in Rome, but he was given no major assignments, in spite of receiving a generous monthly stipend from Giuliano. Instead of doing great art in Rome, Leonardo worked on his scientific studies and designed a machine for the Pope to mint coins. Banking and coin minting had almost disappeared completely in Europe during the Middle Ages; at the time of the Renaissance, both were slowly coming back. Surprisingly, the invention of the printing press led first to advancements in minting coins, rather than printing bills. Leonardo used the same principles from the printing press (which had borrowed ideas from grape presses) to develop his machine to mill coins – a method that led to greater uniformity in size and weight.[86]

---

[86] *Milled coins also made it more difficult to "shave" the edges of coins.*

Final Years - Leonardo in France

King Francis I's comment about Leonardo da Vinci:
"… did not believe that there had ever been another man born into the world who had known so much as Leonardo, and this not only in matters concerning Sculpture, Painting and Architecture, but because he was a great Philosopher."

Leonardo accepted the French King's invitation, and in 1516, he left Italy for good, going to France to be the *Premier Painter and Engineer and Architect of the King.* He lived in a chateau, in Amboise, near the king's palace, receiving a generous annual stipend from his new patron. He was treated almost like a guest, and Leonardo's primary job was to have intellectual discussions with the king! Occasional scientific and architectural studies filled some of his time there as well.

Even though he suffered from a stroke during this time, these last years of his life were the easiest for him. At Leonardo's death, he apologized to "God and Man for leaving so much undone." He died at Amboise in 1519.

Stories vary as to whether Francis I was present when Leonardo died. His earliest biography had the king at Leonardo's side when Leonardo died. Later sources said this was impossible since the king was in another part of France at the time.[87]

---

[87] *And even later, sources said the king was not elsewhere and **could** have been with Leonardo!*

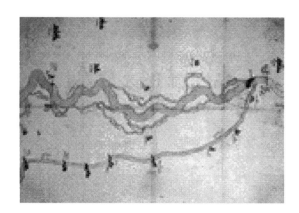

Conclusion

Leonardo da Vinci was a fascinating man, who did fascinating work in a wide variety of areas. For a time, his reputation was of being someone who didn't complete what he started, and that certainly was one of his problems. But in the end, he accomplished much. And what he did accomplish set the stage for many that came after him.

He was the earliest of the "High Renaissance" artists – and one of the better known. Through him, we can gain a better understanding of the times he lived in, as well as of him and his work.

Leonardo is often thought of as a great artist. And he certainly was that. But he was so much more – a dreamer who looked so far beyond the obvious – an architect, a mathematician, a scientist, a musician, and more!

I hope this brief introduction to Leonardo da Vinci, enabled you to learn more about him and his incredible work.

Appendix A - Leonardo's "Vitruvian Man"

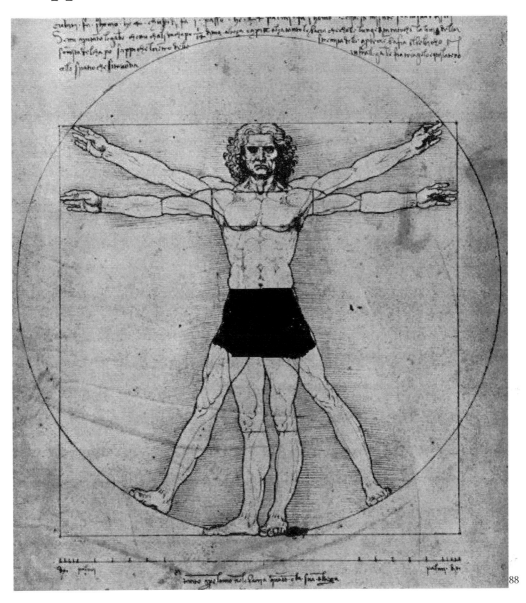

Leonardo da Vinci drew his "Vitruvian Man" to demonstrate the ideal proportions of the human body. Leonardo was not the first to come up with this idea – Vitruvius, a Roman architect and engineer 1400 years before Leonardo, had come up with similar measurements – Leonardo took it to the next "logical" step, and drew the man he was describing. The charts on the next two pages show some of the proportions Leonardo had derived.

---

[88] *Okay, so his Vitruvian Man wasn't clothed. You can find copies of the original elsewhere if you desire it – This is the one I give my students!*

Appendix B - Human Proportions According to da Vinci

(See illustration on previous page and fill-in chart on following page.)

Some interesting observations, made by Leonardo of "similar proportions":

Between shoulder bones	Between hip bones		
Mouth to bottom of Chin	Big toe	1/6 of foot	
From wrist to elbow, and elbow to armpit (when arm is bent).		Length of one foot	
From the fissure (opening) of the mouth, to the bottom of nose		1/7 of the face	
The mouth to the bottom of the chin	The mouth's length	1/4 of the face	
The end of the eye socket (towards the ear), to your ear	The length of the ear	1/3 of the face	The bottom of the chin, to bottom of the nose
The middle of the nose to the bottom of chin		1/2 of the face	
The eyebrows to the bottom of the chin		2/3 of the face	
Beginning of hair to the bottom of the chin	The hand	1/10 of height	
One hand	1/3 of the arm	1/9 of height	
Full head		1/8 of height	
The foot	Face	1/7 of height	
Top of the chest to the crown (top) of the head		1/6 of height	
From elbow to the wrist		1/5 of height	
The max width of the shoulders	The sole of foot to lower edge of knee	1/4 of height	Top of head to middle of chest
Arms out full length		Full height	

While the similarities he "discovered" don't hold true on each individual person, they are close in a surprising number of cases.

Actual Measurements Compared to Leonardo's Predictions:

Measurements in inches or centimeters	Name	Name	Name	Name	Name	Name
Height = Arm span						
Kneeling = 3/4 Height						
Elbow to Wrist = 1/5 Height						
Foot = Face = 1/7 Height						
Middle of nose to bottom of chin = 1/2 Face						
Mouth to bottom of chin = 1/4 Face						

Explanation: Measure body section, listed in each section of chart. Calculate each of the fractions shown (3/4 Height, 1/2 Face, etc.)

Compare – do the measurements in each section = the calculated ones Leonardo predicted? (Typically, some do, and some don't.)

You may want to copy the chart and fill it out with your family or class.

Appendix C
Leonardo's Early Years (Anchiano, Vinci, and Florence)

Dates:	Events in Leonardo's Life:	Related Events:	World Events:
1452	Leonardo's Birth at **Anchiano**, two miles from **Vinci** – He lived there with his mother for his early years.		
1453		Constantinople falls to the Ottoman Turks, bringing an end to the Byzantine Empire.	*Hundred Years' War* between France and England finally ends.
~1455	Leonardo moves to **Vinci** to live with Grandparents.		First Gutenberg Bible printed.
~1466	Moves to **Florence** with his father to apprentice in Andrea Verrocchio's workshop.		Birth of Desiderius Erasmus.
1469		Birth of Nicolo Machiavelli in Florence; Giuliano de Medici becomes new ruler of Florence.	
1472	Leonardo paints angel in Verrocchio's *Baptism of Christ* (left hand corner); also accepted into Painters' Guild that year.		Dante's *Divine Comedy* is printed.
1473	Landscape Drawing, his oldest surviving drawing.		Birth of Nicolaus Copernicus.

Dates:	Events in Leonardo's Life:	Related Events:	World Events:
1475		Birth of Michelangelo	
1476	Leonardo's first younger sibling is born.	Birth of Cesare Borgia (his father will later become Pope Alexander VI). Galeazzo Sforza is assassinated in Milan.	
1477	Starts own workshop; Commissioned for altar-piece for chapel. (Contract almost passed to someone else in 1483!)	Lorenzo de Medici[89] takes power in Florence, after his brother Guiliano's death.	
1480	Leonardo works for Lorenzo de Medici[90].	Ludovico Sforza takes power in Milan.	Birth of Ferdinand Magellan.
1481	Commissioned for *Adoration of the Magi*, first large painting – which like so many others, he leaves unfinished!	Florentine painters go to Rome to decorate Sistine Chapel.	
1482	Leonardo offers service as engineer, architect, sculptor… to Duke of Milan, in famous letter.	Euclid's book *Elements* printed in Latin for first time.	

---

[89] *"Lorenzo the Magnificant"*
[90] *Lorenzo was a patron of the arts, like his father and grandfather before him.*

Milan Years

Dates:	Leonardo's Life:	Related Events:	World Events:
1483	Moves to **Milan;** contracted for first *Virgin of the Rocks*, doesn't finish; starts equestrian statue for Duke of Milan.[91]	Birth of Raphael.	Martin Luther is born in Germany.
1484 & 1485		Plagues in Milan.	
1488	First Anatomical drawings appear in his notebooks.	Duke considers finding another sculptor for his equestrian statue. Verrocchio dies.	
1490	Leonardo directs feasts and pageants; starts serious work in notebooks; sketches plan for *Treatise on Painting*; makes scale model for statue; considers making a telescope.		
1492		Lorenzo de Medici dies; all of Florence attends funeral.	Christopher Columbus discovers America.
1493	Builds full-scale clay model of equestrian statue, unveiled for wedding.	Maximilian I becomes Holy Roman Emperor, and marries Bianca Sforza, daughter of Duke of Milan.	
1494	Paints second *Virgin of the Rocks;* begins construction of canal and molds for statue. He also spends some time in **Pavia** studying.	Sforza family "invites" French King Charles VIII, who invades Italy; Medici family falls from power in Florence. / Machiavelli enters public office in Florence. / Luca Pacioli writes book on accounting methods.	

---

[91] *i.e., he begins initial sketches!*

Dates:	Leonardo's Life:	Related Events:	World:
1495	Begins *Last Supper* in dining room at the Santa Maria delle Grazie (finishes in 1497). Also teaches himself Latin and sketches a robot.	Donato Bramante works on dome for Santa Maria delle Grazie.	
1496		Luca Pacioli comes to Milan to teach mathematics.	Copernicus studies in Italy.
1497	Pacioli works on geometry book, *On Divine Proportion*. Leonardo illustrates it.		
1498	Leonardo plans to publish his notebooks; writes book on theory of mechanics. He meets with other artists to discuss artistic theories.	Louis XII becomes King of France. (Pope annuls Louis' marriage, and arranges for Pope's son, Cesare Borgia, to marry French princess.)	
1499	Leonardo's clay horse is destroyed by French soldiers invading Milan.	Duke Ludovico is driven out of Milan by French troops. Borgia begins subduing Italian cities, with the French King, Louis XII.	Ottoman Empire wages war against Venice (1499 – 1501).

Travel Years

Dates:	Leonardo's Life:	Related Events:	World Events:
1500	Leonardo leaves Milan after it falls to French; he stays briefly in **Mantua**; makes short visit to **Venice** before returning to Florence. Begins 10-year work on *Madonna and Child with St Anne. Last Supper* is already deteriorating.	Cesare Borgia enters Rome as the conqueror of Romagna. (Caterina Sforza is one of the conquered leaders.) Machiavelli visits French king, Louis XII, to enlist aid for Florence's fight against Pisa.	
1501	Sketch for *Madonna and Child with St. Anne* exhibited.	Borgia made Duke of Romagna by the Pope.	Michelangelo is in Rome.
1502	Leonardo serves as military engineer and cartographer to Cesare Borgia; traveling with the army throughout **Romagna**. / Designs bridge for the Sultan.	Machiavelli serves as envoy to Cesare Borgia. Cesare subdues more central Italian cities.	France and Spain are at war with each other.
1503	Returns to **Florence** to great honors. Commissioned for painting of *Battle of Anghiari*; begins *Mona Lisa* (working off and on on both). He also works on plans for canal from Florence to the sea and experiments with flying.	Machiavelli is in Rome for the election of the new Pope, Julius II, after death of Pope Alexander VI. Borgia is poisoned. French defeated in Italy. Machiavelli returns to Florence.	
1504	Leonardo's father dies, leaving behind twelve children, and no will. [92] Leonardo receives nothing from the estate.	Raphael moves to Florence, studies with Leonardo (and later Michelangelo).	Michelangelo finishes *David* sculpture.

[92] *A member of the legal profession., who should have known better.*

Dates:	Leonardo's Life:	Related Events:	World Events:
1505	Finishes full-size sketch of *Battle* painting; does many nature sketches.	Michelangelo starts *Battle of Cascina* on wall across from Leonardo; but is called to Rome before he finishes his painting.	
1506	Summoned to **Milan** by the French governor of the city; stops work on *Battle* painting;[93] finishes *Mona Lisa*.		
1507	Brief trip back to **Florence** plans again to publish notebooks. Uncle dies, leaving everything to Leonardo.		
1508	Returns to **Milan,** where he is employed by French King Louis XII, currently living there. Asked to make statue for victor in Milan, Trivulzio. Begins major anatomical research.	Pope Julius II and Emperor Maximilian I form an alliance.	Michelangelo begins work on ceiling of Sistine Chapel. (Finishes in 1512)

[93] *The summons was not the reason he stopped the battle painting, problems with the painting were.*

Final Years

Dates:	Leonardo's Life:	Related Events:	World Events:
1509			Henry VIII becomes King of England.
1510			Martin Luther visits Rome.
1512		Medici family back in power in Florence, after Swiss defeat French in Italy with help of Pope Julius II's Holy Roman League.	
1513	Leonardo goes to **Rome** at request of Pope Leo X's brother, Giuliano. He opens art studio but concentrates on his science work.	French leave Italy; Machiavelli is imprisoned, released, and then writes *The Prince*. Leo X becomes next Pope.	Raphael and Michelangelo are busy painting in Rome.
1514	Back in Florence for a short time, draws only known self-portrait.[94]	Francis I becomes King of France.	
1515	Travels to **Pavia, Bologna,** and **Milan.** Constructs mechanical lion for Francis I's coronation; is forbidden by Pope from doing more human dissections. Paints last known picture: *St John the Baptist.*	Guiliano de Medici leaves Rome, dies soon afterwards.	

[94] *Shown on the Front Cover. (Some historians list the date as 1512.) Some art historians even debate whether it was actually a self-portrait.*

Dates:	Leonardo's Life:	Related Events:	World Events:
1516	Leonardo moves to **Amboise, France** to work for King Francis I as "Premier Painter and Engineer and Architect of the King." His right hand is paralyzed by a stroke.		Charles V becomes king of Spain. Sir Thomas More publishes *Utopia*.
1517			Martin Luther's *95 Theses* on the Church door.[95]
1519	Leonardo writes his will on April 23rd, dies on May 2nd.		Ferdinand Magellan begins expedition around the world. Hernando Cortez lands in Mexico.

---

[95] *The Reformation begins with this event.*

After Leonardo's Life

Dates:	Related Events:
1550	Giorgio Vasari writes his first edition of *Lives of the Artists*, which includes the first biography of Leonardo da Vinci.
1570	Melzi, one of Leonardo's students, dies, before finishing work on Leonardo's *Treatise on Painting*. Dispersion of the pages of Leonardo's notebooks begins.
1651	Leonardo's *Treatise on Painting* is finally published.
1652	A door is cut in the wall where the *Last Supper* is.
1796	French soldiers deface *Last Supper*.
1797	*Mona Lisa* moved to the Louvre, from Versailles.
1800 — 1803	*Mona Lisa* hangs in Napoleon's bedroom.
1836 & 1845	Bridges finally built where Leonardo had planned one, across mouth of Black Sea.
1911	*Mona Lisa* is stolen.
1913	*Mona Lisa* recovered.
1963	*Mona Lisa* visits U.S.
1974	*Mona Lisa* is encased in a special bullet proof glass box before she visits Tokyo and Moscow, and then returns to France "for good."
1977	Major restoration begins on *The Last Supper*. Idea for *Leonardo's Horse* comes to Charles Dent, in the U.S.
1990's	A Robot is built according to Leonardo's drawings.
1999	Restoration of *The Last Supper* is completed. *Leonardo's Horse* is unveiled in Milan. A working parachute, based on Leonardo's plans, is built and tried out.
2002	*Leonardo's Bridge* is built in Norway.

Appendix D - Leonardo's Contemporaries (1452 – 1519)

- Johannes Gutenberg (1398-1468) – inventor of the Western printing press
- Pope Alexander VI, born "Rodrigo Borgia" (1431 – 1503)
- Andrea Verrocchio (1435 – 1488) – Italian artist, musician, goldsmith
- Pope Julius II, born "Giulano della Rovere" (1443 – 1513)
- Donato Bramante (1444 – 1514) – Italian architect
- Luca Pacioli (1445 – 1514) – Italian mathematician
- Christopher Columbus (1451 – 1506) – Italian/Spanish explorer
- King Henry VII (1457 – 1509) – King of England
- Maximilian I (1459 – 1519) – Holy Roman Emperor
- King Louis XII (1462 – 1515) – King of France, cousin of King Charles VII
- Desiderius Erasmus (1466-1536) – Dutch reformer
- Niccolo Machiavelli (1469 –1527) – Italian political thinker, author of *The Prince*
- King Charles VIII (1470 – 1498) – King of France
- Albrecht Durer (1471-1528) – German painter, scholar, and author
- Nicolaus Copernicus (1473-1543) – Polish astronomer
- (Buonarroti) Michelangelo (1475-1564) – Italian artist
- Pope Leo X, born "Giovanni de Medici" (1475 – 1521)
- Cesare Borgia (1475 – 1507) – notorious Italian military dictator
- Sir Thomas More (1478-1535) English statesman, wrote *Utopia,* wouldn't recognize King Henry VIII as head of church in England (movie about: *Man for All Seasons*)
- Ferdinand Magellan (1480 – 1521) – Portuguese explorer
- Raphael, born "Raffaello Sanzio" (1483-1520) – another great Italian artist
- Martin Luther (1483-1546) "Father" of the Protestant Reformation
- Hernando Cortez (1485 – 1547) Spanish explorer of the New World
- Titian, born "Tiziano Vecellio" (1477-1576) – Italian artist
- King Henry VIII, King of England (1491 – 1547)
- King Francis I, King of France (1494 – 1547)
- Charles, grandson of Ferdinand and Isabella (1500 – 1558) – ruled as Charles I of Spain, beginning in 1516, and Charles V, Holy Roman Emperor, beginning in 1519.
- Giorgio Vasari (1511 – 1574) Italian artist and author of *Lives of the Artists*

Other noteworthy folks who lived soon after him included:
- Tycho Brahe (1546-1601) – Danish astronomer
- William Shakespeare (1564-1616) – English author
- Galileo (1564-1642) – Italian scientist

Appendix E - Bibliography – Books & Web pages

Leonardo da Vinci, General:

Bacci, Mina *Leonardo* Copyright 1978, Fabbri Editori Milan, Italy.

Herbert, Janis *Leonardo da Vinci for Kids* Copyright 1998, Chicago Review Press, Inc. Chicago, IL

Langley, Andrew *Leonardo and His Times* Copyright 1999, Dorling Kindersley, Inc., New York, NY

Reti, Ladislao *The Unknown Leonardo* Copyright 1974, McGraw-Hill Book Co. Maidenhead England.

Richter, Jean Paul *The Notebooks of Leonardo Da Vinci Volumes I and II* Copyright 1970, Dover Publications, Inc., NY

Ripley, Elizabeth *Leonardo Da Vinci* Copyright 1952, Oxford University Press, Inc. US.

Vallentin, Antonina *Leonardo Da Vinci* Copyright 1938, The Viking Press, Inc., New York.

Zollner, Frank *Leonardo* Copyright 2001, Taschen Gmbh Germany.

Zubov, V.P., translated by David H. Kraus *Leonardo da Vinci*, Copyright 1968, Barnes & Noble Inc, NY.

http://www.mos.org/leonardo/

http://www.lairweb.org.nz/leonardo/index.html#stages

www.museoscienza.org/english/leonardo

Anatomy: http://mathforum.org/alejandre/frisbie/math/leonardo.html

Art: Da Vinci, Leonardo, edited by Andre Chatel, translated by ellen Callmann. *Leonardo on Art and the Artist* Copyright 1961, Published in 2002 by Dover Publications, NY

Bridge: http://news.bbc.co.uk/2/hi/europe/1630792.stm

Drawings/Sketches:

Da Vinci, Leonardo *Leonardo Drawings, 60 Works by Leonardo da Vinci*, Copyright 1980 Dover Publications, Inc.

http://library.thinkquest.org/3044/

http://europe.cnn.com/2001/WORLD/europe/07/10/uk.vinci/

Horse: Fritz, Jean *Leonardo's Horse* Copyright 2001, G.P. Putnam's Son, Fogelsville, PA.

Inventions: Cooper, Margaret *The Inventions of Leonardo da Vinci* Copyright 1965, Macmillan Company, NY.

Last Supper:

http://arthistory.about.com/gi/dynamic/offsite.htm?site=http://www.ebtx.com/art/art28.htm

Mona Lisa:

Sasson, Donald *Becoming Mona Lisa* Copyright 2001, Harcourt Inc. Orlando, FL

http://www.pbs.org/treasuresoftheworld/mona_lisa/mlevel_1/mtimeline.html

Paintings:

http://www.ibiblio.org/wm/paint/auth/vinci/

http://www.theartgallery.com.au/ArtEducation/greatartists/DaVinci/

"Iron rusts from disuse; stagnant water loses its purity and in cold weather becomes frozen; even so does inaction sap the vigor of the mind."

Leonardo da Vinci

Printed in Poland
by Amazon Fulfillment
Poland Sp. z o.o., Wrocław

31937150R00094